BOUNCING
BACK
A How-to Manual
for Joy with Minimal
Energy Expenditure

D PICHARDO-JOHANSSON, MD

Published by Manhattan Book Group, an imprint of MindStir Media, LLC
447 Broadway | 2nd Floor #354 | New York, NY 10013 | USA
212-634-7677 | www.manhattanbookgroup.com

Printed in the United States of America
ISBN-13: 978-1-7367342-2-3

TABLE OF CONTENTS

WHY THIS BOOK?

YOU DON'T PRACTICE ONCOLOGY FOR FIFTEEN YEARS WITHOUT LEARNING SOMETHING.

'VE ALWAYS ADMIRED THE STRENGTH of oncology patients facing a terrible diagnosis with grace and dignity. But early in my practice, I became fascinated with a subset of them who sustained superb attitudes through the hardest times. These people did experience downs but bounced back from them quickly. And I don't mean they were plastering a smile on their faces. As unbelievable as it sounds, given their challenges, most of the time, they appeared *genuinely* joyful—even more so than many of the healthy and rich medical colleagues around me. It led me to a conclusion that became the inspiration for this book: **Joy and happiness have more to do with our inner resources than our outer circumstances**.

Soon, I noticed an interesting fact: those joyful patients consistently had fewer side effects from treatment, were less likely to quit it, and had a much better response to therapy (and that's a whole different book!) I loved seeing them thrive, but it seemed unfair that patients who were *not* naturally cheerful could be at a disadvantage. So I made it a point to devote some time during every medical visit to help lift the spirits of the patients who were struggling.

It wasn't easy; imagine working with someone with a melancholic nature who is trapped in self-pity after a cancer diagnosis *and* feels miserable due to chemotherapy side effects. But I had experience in the subject of turning attitudes around. When I was nineteen, I learned this art by caring for my mother, my very first cancer patient.

First, with my mother and then with my patients, I'd become a *jujitsu* master of dismantling self-defeating inner arguments, and a teacher of the art of boosting joy even in the grimmest of circumstances. And it worked! Most patients were able to change their outlooks, and that translated into all sorts of improved outcomes. That finding led to the second conclusion that inspired me to write this book: **We're not prisoners of our nature; we can exercise and strengthen the muscles of joy and resilience.**

I applied many of those techniques with great results to my own life setbacks over the years (kids with special needs, life after divorce, health issues, career dilemmas . . .). I became a student of all the different ways to boost joy in my life. I devoted so much time and energy to work on the emotional aspect of my patients' health that I admit sometimes I neglected the business portion—but it was worth it. I felt proud of having perfected the art of lifting others. Or so I thought.

And then *I* was diagnosed with cancer.

Talk about "putting your money where your mouth is." For the roughly one year that it took me to recover my health (three cancer surgeries, chemotherapy, radiation, reconstruction surgery, and re-adjusting to life), I got to test one by one all the self-lifting skills I used to offer my patients and their relatives. My skill set expanded, refined, and perfected beyond what I would've ever planned otherwise. And the best part was I maximized the techniques that require the *minimal possible energy expenditure.* Trust me, if I could apply them while lying in bed, nauseous and exhausted from chemo, anybody can. That led to the third conclusion that caused me to write this book: **You don't have to expend a huge amount of energy to lift yourself up. Very small shifts can cause drastic differences.**

And here comes the best news: I confirmed something I'd suspected all my life. Navigating that storm truly became equivalent to lifting weights with my soul and strengthening its muscles. Every other challenge I've faced in my life since has seemed much smaller. I've got bouncing back and returning to joy down to a system.

Best example? In the midst of the COVID-19 pandemic, I found myself feeling more peaceful than I would've ever imagined, despite the fact that it had coincided with me being without an income after quitting my job and facing conflicts in my family life the quarantine made resurface. I sailed through the storms trusting that everything would turn out all right. This book was born during those days.

I invite you to dive into this book with a smile and an open mind. You might find it puzzling at times, but trust me, hang in there and keep a sense of humor. I promise to make it worth your while. You'll probably get out of it something completely different from what you think you will. But I guarantee you, you'll be a different—happier—person by the end.

PART I:
HOW TO APPROACH THIS BOOK

NO TIME TO WASTE

I FIND IT ANNOYING WHEN I read a new book, and the author takes forever to get to the point. Come on! My time is valuable; I'm sure yours is too. Balancing a practice, four children, a husband, support groups, and a passion for writing, I'm highly selective about how I invest my time.

And there's another small detail that makes me picky: I'm a recent cancer survivor. So no, there's no time to waste here.

Being a physician, I could've started the book by quoting research that supports the importance of joy in our health. Or I could've rambled about the difference between *authentic* joy and the art of plastering a fake smile on your face. Instead, I'll start with the essential parts. If you only read the first five chapters, you'll be in better shape and equipped with great tools to confront challenges.

Of course, I strongly encourage you to read the whole book, as I firmly believe its simple hacks will make a drastic difference in your ability to bounce back from adversity and feel joy in all aspects of your life. But here's the secret: It is okay to cherry-pick and skip some parts that don't apply to you. Make sure to complete the first section and then follow my pointers so you can get the best possible experience from this read.

STORIES

I'm a storyteller (a novelist), so this book will be loaded with stories, many of them personal. Those are real, but, of course, I've changed names and details for privacy. The very first story will be the sequence of life experiences that led me to write this book so you can get to know me a little better. (First time-saving trick: if you've already decided to trust me and don't need convincing that I know what I'm talking about, it's okay to skip that chapter or return to it later).

EXERCISES

Throughout this book, I'll be assigning you practical exercises. To get the most out of these sessions, I recommend you devote a notebook or journal to them—writing something reinforces learning it.

STRUCTURE

In Part I of this book, we'll work on something that I consider the best investment we can make: learning to raise your joy baseline. In Part II, we will touch on how to bounce back from setbacks. In Part III, we'll discuss troubleshooting and additional tools, and in Part IV, we'll bring this knowledge home and apply it to different life challenges. Here's another secret: *It is okay to skim* over some of those sections that don't apply to you. If one of them seems particularly pertinent to your current situation, feel free to read that part first, but I still believe you'll get the best out of it if you've read sections in order.

Another situation when it's advisable to break the order of this book: If at any point you feel stuck in a section, I invite you to go to the chapters on troubleshooting and see if one of the topics described there applies to you.

An important note: In this book, I'll be using some controversial words such as "God," "The Universe," and "Spirituality." Please do not let those turn you off. If you're reading this on a physical book, feel free to take a pen and scratch them all over (or use electronic tools to make notes on an e-book). Go ahead and replace them with words you feel more comfortable with: "Higher power" instead of God. "God" instead of Universe, "Religion" or "Ethics" instead of Spirituality . . .

Full disclosure, I was raised religious but currently consider myself mostly a deeply spiritual person. What does that mean to me? I seek to achieve a deep connection with the Divinity every day through many different vehicles—love and service to others, daily prayer and meditation, communion with nature, listening to inspirational speakers I resonate with—but I no longer follow a specific religious group or attend a weekly service. If you want to scratch the word Spiritual and replace it with "hippie," it's okay. (That was a joke).

FINAL DISCLAIMER

I've made an effort to write this book not as a physician, but as a human being who's learned through facing life challenges and has something to share. I won't insult your intelligence by writing a two-page disclosure reminding you, "this is not intended to be medical advice."

Still, bear with me in the next short section, as I comply with an obligatory disclaimer. I'm not allowed to tell you that you can skip this part (but you know you can). Instead, I've tried to give it a fun twist by sharing a glimpse at one of my most important sources of joy and support in my life: my husband, David.

IMPORTANT. READ THIS. THE OBLIGATORY DISCLAIMER (YADA-YADA)

My beloved husband David, a brilliant professor of English and an author, absolutely hates the sentence, *"If this is a medical emergency, please hang up and dial 911."*

"Oh, come on! Why are they wasting my time repeating that?" David protests, rolling his eyes, every time he calls some doctor's office and the same darn recording plays again. "Doesn't *everybody* on the whole planet know by now they have to call 911 for an emergency?"

David has little patience for wasting time because he's a connoisseur of life with many diverse interests. He's my joy and pleasure guru and probably the smartest man I've ever met. (Yes, among the medical and scientific communities I've frequented, I might've met men who technically have higher IQs than David. But he takes the gold because, unlike the narrow-interested scientist, he has a multi-faceted intelligence. But I digress.)

My point is, I understand David. I would never insult him (or *you*, my smart reader) by repeating this warning over and over again throughout this book. But I'm legally obligated to say it at least once. I will just phrase it in a more respectful way than the automatic recording. Here it goes:

If, at any moment during this book, your gut feeling tells you you're not safe, *get help.*

You are smart. You know yourself better than anyone else. If you realize we're about to dig into feelings that are getting way too uncomfortable, and you may lose grip, or if you are despairing and having ideas about death, GO GET HELP. Ideally, get professional help. But at least reach for someone you love, somebody you know who cares about you, or at least someone you trust to decide whether or not to take you to a hospital. Reach for them and say, "I don't feel safe right now. Please help me."

In this book, I have purposefully avoided discussing anti-depressants because, despite me being a physician, it is not intended to replace medical therapy. The strategies in this book will help you whether you are on medical therapy or not.

And in case of an emergency, there's always 911 or the National Suicide Prevention Lifeline: 1-800-273-8255.

1

WHO I AM. MY STORY OF SURVIVAL

ONCE DECIDED I WOULD BE the best freaking oncologist in the whole world.

I was nineteen and already on a fast track to getting a medical degree when my mother was diagnosed with incurable cancer. It was multiple myeloma, a disease that currently has a great prognosis, but back then had few treatment options.

A giant of fortitude, my mother recovered quickly from the shock of the news and was often the one offering my father, my sisters, and me support and encouragement. One afternoon, after returning from a radiation appointment for her broken arm, we chatted of nothing in particular, mostly trying to make sense of the mess of our shaken lives, when she said, "You're taking such good care of me; I can already see you being a wonderful doctor in the future."

At that moment, I didn't know she would beat the odds and still be alive four and a half years later. I treasured every sentence that came off her lips as if it could potentially be the last words I'd hear from her. (Which, by the way, is exactly how we should listen to every person we love every day.)

So I never forgot the words that came next, "Maybe it is true that everything happens for a reason. Maybe my diagnosis had to happen in order to define the type of doctor you'll be in the future."

I took her words literally. I graduated from medical school with maximum honors and pursued an internal medicine specialty at Wayne State University in Detroit, which opened the doors of Northwestern University in Chicago for my hematology-oncology fellowship and my master's in clinical investigation. I had many ambitious dreams at the time. I would work in research and contribute to finding the cure for cancer. I would leave a mark in the United States and eventually bring that knowledge to help cancer patients in the Dominican Republic, where my family is from.

When my children's health issues peaked and time became an even larger issue, I had to narrow my focus and decided patient care would be my priority. I chose a clinical path over research and academics, but that didn't reduce the size of my dreams. My contribution to the world would be the love I'd give each patient. I would bring to the career the compassion and empathy that only someone who'd lost a loved one from cancer could bring.

For the next years, I fell passionately in love with my cancer patients. I poured my whole being into helping cure those who could be cured, give a quality of life to those who couldn't, and ensure the most painless transition for those who'd lose the battle. I was determined to make a difference. If anything, to prove that my mother's suffering had not been in vain.

Fast-forward a decade, and I had nothing left to give. Every patient I had lost carved a scar in my heart, leaving me exhausted, heartbroken, and raw. And to soothe my guilt about so many people I'd been unable to help, I had to stop taking any credit for those who did survive. I found myself trapped in a hostile environment, surrounded by physicians who saw each other as fierce competitors, where the corporate side of the business made it clear that the bottom line of all our work was not patient care but profit.

By then, I admitted that I'd decided to pursue oncology at one of the lowest points of my life, shortly after my mother's death—the same time when I'd also decided to marry my now ex-husband. At the time, these felt like the right choices, but those decisions matched the person I used to be—broken, drained, and hurting. Continuing to bind myself to those decisions meant perpetuating that identity. Through the process of reinventing myself after divorce and finding love with my current husband, I'd learned the importance of letting go of what wasn't working.

But there was more! Usually, my family life infused me strength, but at the time of my career crisis, it added another stress. My daughter, Irene, suffered frequent seizures that might indicate a life-threatening neurological condition and explain her special needs. At moments I felt as if God was hitting me from all directions. Being the only thing I could control, I prepared to take the financial penalty for breaking my contract and quit my oncology job.

And then, I was diagnosed with *two* cancers.

Here, the oncologist in me feels obligated to clarify, "It's not as bad as it sounds." One of them was a bread-and-butter, early-stage invasive breast carcinoma that I knew from the beginning was curable. The second one—a much more rare form of ectopic cancer—posed more of a treatment challenge with a less clear prognosis. But even that proved treatable. Compared to some of the devastating cases I'd treated over my career, this was manageable.

Still, recovering my health required extensive work. My plans to leave my job had to be placed on hold, as this was not the right time to change insurances. For the next year, I embraced each step with all my being.

- Double mastectomies.
- Two additional margin excision surgeries.
- Chemotherapy.
- Losing my hair.
- Premature menopause from the chemo.
- Radiation.
- Reconstruction surgery.
- Hormone blocker therapy.

My mother's words from long ago resounded in my mind. "Maybe it is true that everything happens for a reason." Perhaps this experience was the missing piece to give my career a second chance, to offer me a new perspective. Maybe I would be able to help cancer patients even more after becoming one.

Did that happen? Well, I will not give you spoilers. You'll have to keep reading.

I will tell you that these trials stretched me to a new level of spiritual and psychological growth. Every survival strategy and every resilience tool I'd ever acquired through my life ripened and fell into place. From navigating the care of a mother with cancer to the brutal world of surviving medical school and residency training. From dealing with children with severe health issues and special needs to escaping an oppressive marriage. From the joys of finding love against all prognoses to the courage to admit that the career I devoted my life to no longer made me happy.

But enough about me; this book is about *you*. If you don't read one more page after this, take this message with you as the essence of this book: *Life is a perfectly orchestrated experience.* Every setback you've ever encountered has been a nudge toward a better life. Every hardship you've endured has been an exercise of lifting weights with your soul that will bring you countless blessings in the future—from personal joy to the ability to bring joy to someone else who's going through a difficult moment. I intend that by the end of our journey together, you'll walk away with the strength and inner resources to manage anything life throws at you.

Okay. Are you ready? Let's begin.

2

RAISING OUR BASELINE AND LEARNING TO LEVEL OURSELVES

THE IMPORTANCE OF MINDING OUR MOOD

Have you noticed how everyday challenges are easier or harder to navigate depending on our mood? If we're upset, even the smallest mishap irritates us. If we're feeling well, we can let even big issues slide. Let's use the most typical example.

One morning, you get up from bed and stub your toe on a toy truck your kid left on the floor. The sore toe puts you in a bad mood, and you're cranky and distracted and spill coffee on your shirt. Now you need to change your shirt, which delays you, causing you to get stuck in rush hour traffic. Your boss gives you a bad look about your delay, so you snap at a coworker; the morning spirals down from there.

On the other hand, imagine a morning when you're in a particularly good mood. The best example is being newly in love. Nothing can spoil your joy. Not only would you care less about the small nuisances such as stubbing your toe, spilling some coffee, or running into traffic, I dare say you'll be less likely to encounter them.

Doesn't it feel that when we're in a great mood, the world seems to perform better for us? All the traffic lights seem to be green. All the solutions we need appear to present themselves. If it has been a long time since you last had a truly blissful day, I don't blame you for being skeptical. For now, take my word for it.

This phenomenon of how good luck seems to perpetuate itself while a bad mood triggers more bad things to happen is not a coincidence. New Age thinkers call it "being in or out of alignment," or "putting out a vibration that attracts what's in your mind." If you don't subscribe to those terms, I invite you to look at it more scientifically. Facing a hardship (in this case, stubbing a toe) puts us in the "survival" mode, flooding us with adrenaline and engaging the oldest parts of the brain (such as the amygdala and the limbic system). No wonder solutions evade us, and we get caught in knee-jerk over-reactions and fight-or-flight responses, causing blunders to pile one on top of the other.

Instead, to face day-to-day challenges, we want to operate from our *pre-frontal cortex*, the more mature and sophisticated brain region which we have and animals lack, that is capable of very complex decisions. And this is even more critical anytime we face extraordinary life challenges—from career burnout to divorce to a scary diagnosis. Then, it's more important than ever to become watchdogs of our good mood. We need to defend our inner peace with any weapon possible and the commitment of Rambo. If you don't read one more page in this book, let this be the most important message: Fire the negative people in your life. If you can't fire them, reduce your interaction with them to the minimum. I used to tell my patients, "Make me the bad guy. Tell those people, 'I'm sorry, but my oncologist has forbidden me to engage in anything that upsets me. I have to end this conversation now.'" You have my permission to use me as an excuse. Tell your energy-draining friends, "I'm sorry, but I'm reading this book, and this doctor who's an expert in joy and love says I'm not allowed to talk to anybody who stresses me out."

If we could identify the moment when our moods are about to go downhill and put a halt to it, we would be much more likely to do damage control and continue coasting throughout our days. For that, we need a handle on two things: we need to create *a good baseline,* and we need to master *the art of bouncing back* fast from setbacks. Here we'll focus on the first step, and we'll touch on bouncing back in the following chapters.

CREATING A GOOD BASELINE

Allow me to nerd out for a minute. Human organisms are truly walking miracles. Everything in your body is designed to restore balance once it is lost and to return to normal values—your *baseline*. If you go for a run on a hot day and sweat profusely, a region of your brain called the hypothalamus will sense that you need water and will stimulate the production of hormones to make you thirsty. Once you've drunk enough to bring the plasma volume and sodium concentration back to normal, your thirst will mitigate. If you overshoot, antidiuretic hormone levels will go down, making you urinate the excess water.

For this chain of complex feedback loops to work, we need a working sensor (in this case, the hypothalamus) that has recorded what *normal* means and will work toward restoring that value. In an ideal, healthy body, that sensor has been programmed with the healthiest value. If illness occurs (hypertension, diabetes insipidus, syndrome of inappropriate ADH . . .), the body would be set for a wrong target, and all our body resources will be working toward keeping that abnormal value.

Guess what? Our psyches are also like that; they're set to a favorite feeling. In an ideal situation, that favorite feeling is joy or contentment. But blame it on habit or childhood trauma, more often than not, that baseline is a negative emotion. For some people, their baseline is being angry all the time. Some seem to have sadness as their base camp, or constant stress and fear. In addition to a favorite mode, our minds will also be programmed for an intensity or degree of that feeling. Let's call it our "Mood Thermostat." An event can temporarily knock us down from our favorite mood state, but give it time, and the tendency will be to return to it.

Can we change our Mood Thermostat if we don't like what it is? Yes. One of the most effective ways is psychotherapy to process life traumas and childhood hurts. But that is a lengthy commitment you may or may not be willing to embark on right now. This book offers much simpler, effective hacks you can apply immediately to re-wire your brain. As a busy professional and mother of four, I'm a big advocate of anything that can give me results with minimal time and effort. I like to call it "applying leverage tweaks." Since we've established that this book is written for people without time to waste, let's focus on that.

The entire first section of this book is about raising your baseline or adjusting your Joy Thermostat. To achieve that, we first need to take care of one important step: We need to learn to *read* that Thermostat.

RECONNECTING

Before you can master your emotions, you must learn to read your Thermostat by reconnecting with what you feel.

As we go through life, we learn to disconnect from our feelings for many reasons. We might have created a habit of ignoring what we feel and want. We might've learned to dissociate under stress and view problems as if they're happening to someone else. We might enter acute denial when something bad happens. Getting to the root of those tendencies and healing them would be work beyond the spectrum of this book. For now, I will just invite you to make it a habit to check on yourself regularly. "How am I feeling right now? *For real*." Don't judge it, don't try to fix it, don't even beat yourself too hard if you have the feeling that you're giving an insincere answer. The point is to create a new habit of self-awareness and practice, practice, practice until it becomes second nature to know how we feel at any given time.

If this feels like too big of a task, remember I'm not asking you to do anything about it (yet). You'll just practice the skill of checking on your state of mind until you get the hang of it. If you're the type of person who absolutely hates digging into their feelings, or if this feels like a complete waste of time, I still have tools and hacks you can use instead (read the troubleshooting sections "I'm not into digging" and "I feel numb"). But let's face it: you'll get a lot more from this book if you just humor me and go through the motions. If, after doing all these exercises, you don't feel you got anything from them, you're entitled to send me a nagging email. But I have the feeling you won't.

EXERCISE: READING YOUR THERMOSTAT

Reminder: Ideally, I would like you to devote a notebook or journal for these exercises—writing something reinforces learning it.

This may sound a little crazy (or hippie-dippy), but please bear with me.

1. I want you to imagine your body contains four storage compartments: joy/peace, sadness, anger, and fear. When you evoke a sad memory, where do you feel it in your body? In your chest? In your throat? In your head? Where do you feel your anger? Your sadness?

In my case, I tend to feel most of my feelings in my chest, but in slightly different locations, as if my thorax were sub-divided in spaces. I tend to feel joy and peace in the innermost space, my heart, while sadness feels more like a band in my chest wall—outside the heart, squeezing it. My anger, on the other hand, settles more in the upper chest, closer to the base of my throat, while fear/anxiety gnaws me lower, close to my upper stomach.

Close your eyes and try to feel/imagine where those compartments would be for you.

2. Done? Write that down or draw a diagram if you prefer. Don't worry if you feel it's an imperfect effort; you can always change it or correct it later.

3. Next, close your eyes and try to feel which of those four feelings best describes your current state. Are you currently anxious? Write "fear." Depressed? Write "sadness." Are you upset with someone right now? Write down "anger"—you get it. If you currently feel numb and can't really feel anything, write *Joy/Peace,* and I'll explain in a minute why.

4. For the next step, I want you to rate that feeling from one to ten. For example, if you're rating fear, ten would be the moment you remember having been the most terrified in your life, and one would be just a small twinge of anxiety. If you're feeling completely numb, I want you to give yourself a zero in the area of joy/peace.

5. And now comes the most important part of the exercise (all the previous steps were just a warm-up). I want you to check the storage compartment for joy in your body—wherever you feel it is—and rate it on a scale from minus ten to positive ten.

Here's how that goes: Minus ten would be feeling so depressed you're suicidal. Zero would be complete numbness, and ten would be euphoria.

Right now, I would rate my joy at a positive eight point five. Why so high? This is one of my favorite moments in the day: when everyone else in the house still sleeps, and I'm writing. You can say I'm a morning person. I woke up well-rested. The caffeine from my morning coffee is kicking in along with the blood sugar of my breakfast (high blood levels of the hormone cortisol, which peaks in early morning, also help). If I'm feeling so joyous, why not a ten? Well, I reserve the ten score for moments of true euphoria, like the blast of joy you feel after a piece of great news. It's usually brief and sometimes can even be uncomfortable to sustain for me (call it my glass ceiling), so I tend to aim at a nine. Right now, I'm almost at a nine, but not quite because I have a couple of errands to run and those are getting my attention in the back of my mind. Still, eight point five is great, and I'll take it any day.

Of course, my ten and someone else's ten would differ, as they depend on subjective experiences. The best part of this approach is that you can't get it wrong. *You* are the only expert on *you*. So you don't have to compare yourself to anyone else.

6. The last part of the exercise is to try to get the hang of what your baseline is. What feeling seems to predominate most days? What is your most common joy score? You may already know the answer to these questions, or you may want to keep a record over the next few days to get a better idea. Again, there is no judgment here. We need to know where we're starting in order to know how to take us to the next level.

3
RETRAINING THE BRAIN

MY BOY AND GIRL TWINS are the cutest, most loving, funniest kids you'll ever meet. They have a passionate love-hate relationship, and watching them interact is pure fun. They look nothing like each other (he's fair with green eyes, while she's dark and exotic), yet they're both stunning.

And they also have different degrees of special needs.

My daughter has several developmental delays and autism. Her twin has milder learning challenges and falls on the spectrum to a milder degree. Before I had them, both my older boys needed speech therapy for a while. So, I've spent my parenthood years training myself in speech and developmental therapy and how to re-wire the brain. It's amazing how much of that information can apply to retraining our brains as adults.

One of the concepts I loved when working with my kids was the concept of floor-time play therapy to create new brain synapses. Sitting on the floor with the child, playing games of his or her choice, and introducing small challenges one at a time, we created new brain circuits and pathways. Call it brain re-habilitation. The human brain is amazingly pliable. Even if the neurons (the nervous system cells) cannot regenerate once damaged, cells all around the damaged ones are capable of picking up the function and compensate by creating new connections—new synapses. To illustrate this, I'll share a real story that inspired me greatly when working with my kids.

I met a patient, and I'll call him Sam, who'd once been sent to hospice after a massive stroke. The stroke had left him paralyzed, only barely able to move his right hand. By the time I met him, he was walking without a cane and speaking fluently, so I asked him how he had recovered.

"I assumed I was going to die soon," he told me. "So I asked my wife to move us close to the ocean. She sold everything we had and bought a tackle and bait store. I used to sit in my wheelchair behind the counter, next to her, just watching people come and go, unable to move.

"Then one day, I saw a fishing hook on the counter and thought, 'I'm just going to grab that.' I let my fingers slowly crawl on the counter until I could reach it. The first time it took me forever, but I kept practicing again and again. And little by little, I started gaining my strength back."

Wouldn't it be wonderful if we could also rehab the part of our brains that handle our psychology? The good news is that we can. Later on, I ran into a lecture from *New York Times* bestselling author and psychologist Dr. Rick Hanson, talking about a related concept that has fascinated me ever since: Neuroplasticity.

NEUROPLASTICITY

Sam's story becomes more admirable by pointing out a medical fact: In the adult brain, neurons don't have the ability to reproduce and regenerate like, for example, our skin cells. For Sam to recover, he didn't "grow new neurons" to replace the dead areas, but instead other, different regions of his brain re-wired and took over those brain functions. The brain's ability to make new connections and change the way it's wired is called neuroplasticity.

In the same way we can create new connections in the brain to recover from a stroke, we can create new connections and strengthen others to rehab paths of happiness and optimism. The way to achieve this is to pay attention to positive experiences that would otherwise go unnoticed during our day and make sure we *take them in* by savoring the moment for ten to twenty seconds. Think of it as pressing the record button. According to the theory of neuroplasticity, every time we do, we strengthen those underdeveloped neuropaths.

While Sam's amazing recovery isn't a typical story, it illustrates how resilient the human brain can be. I believe that, even after severe emotional trauma, new brain pathways can allow us to regain our capacity for joy. Like any rehab program, it takes time and consistency, but it can truly shift the way we see the world. Many of the concepts we'll discuss in this book are based on that approach.

A JOY DIET

Another concept that fascinates me about giving therapy to children with special needs is the sensory diet. Children with special needs, especially kids on the autistic spectrum, struggle to integrate the sensory input they receive. Many kids crave some sensations to soothe themselves, for example, spinning around or putting objects in their mouths. Some strongly reject others, such as loud noises. As part of my kids' occupational therapy, we ensured that they had a large dose of the soothing sensations they craved every day. That led to a more relaxed child, more open to learning. At the same time, we stretched the kid's tolerance by exposing them to small amounts of the sensations they feared, allowing them to desensitize to them little by little.

You might be asking, "What does this have to do with me?" Please bear with me.

That concept of the sensory diet made a huge difference in my children's recovery, both for my older boys' mild speech delays, which resolved completely, and later on for their sister's autism. For my oldest son, running around and roughhousing worked best. My father described it as "getting the heebie-jeebies out of him." My daughter prefers swimming and endless hours swinging at the playground.

This got me thinking: with all the challenges adult life throws at us, doesn't it make sense that we create our own self-soothing techniques? And I don't mean only physical activity, which releases endorphins in the blood to improve the mood. I also mean a disciplined schedule of pleasurable activities for the mind and the soul.

God knows we don't need to look far to find problems; sometimes, it feels like life is constantly throwing them at us. But joyful moments? Moments of bliss? Those we have to *actively pursue*. It is our responsibility to make them occur. Then our improved mood will typically make it easier to perpetuate the momentum of joy, especially if we take the opportunity to take those moments in and press the record button to continue rewiring our brain.

The next thing I want you to get out of this book is that we need to give ourselves a steady supply of joyful and soothing experiences during the day. Bestselling author and founder of Mind Movies Natalie Ledwell uses the term "Success Rituals." I like to call it a Joy Diet. Just in the same way we made it a routine to brush our teeth every day, shower, and eat, we can learn to make sacred, non-negotiable habits out of activities that improve our quality of life.

Here you may sigh and say, "Creating new habits is hard for me. I've been trying unsuccessfully for years to stick to—" Fill in the blank with exercising, eating healthy, meditating . . .

Here comes the great news: you're drastically more likely to succeed at sticking to a Joy Diet than to any previous self-improvement effort. This is due to the simple fact that *it will be something deeply enjoyable*. You don't need a doctorate to know that we tend to repeat activities that bring us pleasure and avoid those that bring us pain.

I'm not talking about whipping yourself into a new activity that has to pile on top of your already packed calendar. I'm talking about asking yourself what is that thing you enjoy deeply and haven't done in a while, or what is that one activity you've always wanted to do and haven't.

My best personal experience of a Joy Diet revolves around writing. When I discovered the pleasure of releasing my scientific brain and pouring my wild imagination into fiction plotting, I was reborn. People still ask me, "How on earth did you have time to publish eight novels when you had a full-time job and four kids?" The honest answer is that *I love writing more than I love sleeping.* I'd rise as early as four in the morning to squeeze in my drafting time before my kids and husband woke up—and eagerly looked forward to it. That moment of sipping my coffee and writing in my cozy chair while the house is still quiet is one of my favorite pleasures in the world.

Like my husband David once said about monogamy: "To hell with self-control; you need to *want* to be there. If you're crazy about the person you're with, you don't have to work hard on marital faithfulness." If you love the activity, you won't have to pour energy into forcing yourself to do it.

Joy rehab starts by making sure you have a dose of pleasure at least twice a day to bring your mood back up to a higher baseline, and making sure you take it in. At the end of this chapter, I'll provide you with an exercise to jumpstart your ideas about building a Joy Diet. But first, I will train you to be a joy connoisseur. Just like a fine wine taster knows the difference between a five-dollar and a two-hundred-dollar wine bottle, here I'll guide you to understand the different quality-levels of joy-restoring activities.

JOY-RESTORING ACTIVITIES

Since we're talking about a Joy *Diet*, let's stick to the food metaphor for a little longer. Just like not all foods are created equal, not all joy activities are. Some of them will be highly nutritious and will sustain you for a long time, while others will be comfort food or a sweet treat that will only bring you up for a short time. (Hey, no judgment. We all need a little comfort food from time to time). If you're sincere, you'll recognize that most foods that give you a temporary sugar high will also cause a sugar crash later on that leaves you feeling worse. For example, have you noticed kids after a birthday party, hyper on birthday cake? When they finally crash, they get cranky, cry for a while, and then fall asleep suddenly. The same applies to nourishment for the soul and mind. Binge-watching Netflix can be a quick way to disconnect the brain to avoid confronting what worries us. However, if you overdo it (and you know more than anyone what overdoing it means for you), you'll end the day feeling bad because you spent the afternoon sitting on a couch and didn't accomplish anything productive to solve your problem.

My favorite example of the subtleties of the nutritional value of joy activities is the wide spectrum of reading materials. My husband, an English Literature professor and fellow writer, once expressed his worry that I seemed to have degenerated in my reading. I'd once been his unofficial book-club partner to whom he loved recommending classic literature. Suddenly, for a while, I was reading nothing but "silly romance novels." (No offense intended for fellow romance writers). The fact was, after facing a day of depressing cases in my oncology practice, I could not take any story portraying human suffering, no matter what a masterpiece of the English language it was. I needed to immerse myself in a guaranteed-happy-ending story that didn't require much of a stretch from my brain. A story where the characters are physically perfect and healthy, have tons of sex (often quite explicitly in the novel), and after overcoming their First World problems, find their happily ever after. I have to say that "silly" romance books have saved my life more than once, including giving me company in hospital rooms those countless long nights when my daughter was hospitalized.

But of course, those books are a different breed and no substitute for a great novel with wonderfully crafted characters, vivid descriptions, and an entrancing plot that touches the soul and gives the reader catharsis (more on that later). When I'm not flattened by exhaustion and overwhelmed, I acknowledge that's a more fulfilling way to go.

The truth is that engaging in high-quality joy tasks demands a little more of our stamina, and when we're sunk in deep depression, anxiety, or negativity, we will have little energy to pursue them. Here I propose that we can get ourselves jumpstarted with those favorite quick-fix activities and guilty pleasures, always aiming at raising our bar progressively to favor the higher-quality joy-boosts. My suggestion is to put a time limit to those sweet-treat activities or even reserve them for emergencies when you *really* need a quick boost. In some times of our lives, that would be every day after returning from work exhausted—and that's okay too.

In the following chapter, I will provide lists with suggestions for quick joy fixes as well as examples of much more nourishing activities that can help re-boost your mood in more durable ways. Go over the lists taking notes, and pick the ones that resonate the most strongly with you. Remember, to make it to your personal list, *it has to feel good*. If it doesn't feel great and doesn't leave you wanting to do it again the next day, it doesn't count as a joy activity.

4
THE JOY MENU

STARTING WITH DESSERT

As WE INTRODUCED IN THE last chapter, our Joy Diet will be a mixture of highly nutritious activities and occasional sweet treats or quick fixes. But allow me to improvise a suggestion that goes against our usual traditions: At the dinner table, we reserve dessert for the end, as a sign that the meal is wrapping up. In this list, we will *start* with the sweets. That's because they're the fastest way to jumpstart our mood, bringing us back from the deepest lows. These sweets should still be used sparingly. And once they have lifted us enough to recover some energy, we should use it to engage in one of the more substantial and durable mood-boosting activities.

But first, we have to cover an important warning: anything that gives you a quick brain rush of pleasure can temporarily short-circuit your brain to favor that activity over all others. The most severe form of this physiological response is called addiction. Let's explore that for a minute.

GUILTY PLEASURES VERSUS ADDICTIONS

Any activity that results in mind numbing can potentially become addictive. And the same activity that can be lifesaving for someone could potentially be detrimental for someone else. For example, having a glass of wine while sitting on their back porch at the end of the day might be the ultimate soothing activity for someone, while someone else struggling with alcoholic tendencies urgently needs to avoid it.

In a more personal example: for some times in my life, I used shopping as my brain disconnection activity. That occasionally led to impulse buys and spending money on unnecessary things, but I considered it worth it for the amount of therapy it gave me. However, that activity would be much more destructive for my friend Celia, a self-proclaimed shopaholic who deals with a fifty-thousand-dollar-credit-card debt.

Is being a "shopaholic" an official diagnosis? Not technically. *The Diagnostic and Statistical Manual of Mental Disorders,* 5th edition, or DSM V (the bible for mental health providers), addresses addiction mostly regarding substance disorders. The only behavioral addiction it approaches is gambling. I found a much better definition of addiction in the *International Classification of Disease*, 11th Edition (ICD-11). The World Health Organization's ICD-11 Working Group proposed to approach behavioral addictions as "impulse control disorders." This manual defines them as "repeated failure to resist an impulse, drive, or urge to perform an act that is rewarding to the person (at least in the short-term), *despite longer-term harm either to the individual or to others.*"

Did you catch the part in italics? In my interpretation, as long as your obsession is harmless to you and others, it cannot be categorized as a mental disorder. If you scramble the minimal self-control to avoid negative consequences, you get a free pass. Let's take the example of being obsessed with shopping for designer shoes. If you're spending so much that you're in debt or failing to save for emergencies and retirement, you are technically harming yourself, and it counts as pathological. What if you are not? What if you are a disciplined, hard-working woman who consistently saves money and has no major debt? What if you have proof that the goal of treating yourself to a great pair of shoes encourages you and makes you work harder? Great! You earned your right to shop for shoes compulsively.

The bottom line: *you know yourself better than anybody else.* If any of the activities below is something you tend to binge on to the point of losing control, remove it from your Joy Diet menu. It is also common knowledge that forcing yourself not to think about something doesn't work—when we do that, our brains will automatically fixate on that one thing we're trying to avoid. Instead of focusing on avoiding the activities on the list that you're afraid are detrimental for you, focus on choosing different ones you feel you would enjoy and then pour all your attention onto them.

Call for Action

These lists were created through the filter of my personal experiences and may feel incomplete when applied to you. If you have a joy ritual or recharging activity that really works for you and is not mentioned here, by all means, write it on your list. What's more, email me at pichardojohanssonmd@gmail.com and propose them to be added to the next edition of the book. I will add them and will give you credit in the book's acknowledgments.

AND NOW LET'S GET TO WORK—PREAMBLE TO EXERCISE 2

Take a piece of paper, or even better, a page in your journal. (If you don't have one, I strongly recommend you get one). Make three columns. Number one will be "Mind Candy." Number two will be "Nutritious Activities," and Number three will be "Joy Super Foods." Go over the next lists and write down those that grab your attention—as many as you wish.

After each activity, I elaborate a little to help clarify the point, but feel free to skip that if you're absolutely certain of whether that is a "yes" or a "no" and don't need convincing.

This is worth repeating: Pick the activities that resonate most strongly with you. Remember, *it has to feel good*. If it doesn't feel great and doesn't leave you wanting to do it again the next day, it doesn't deserve to go on your list.

MIND CANDY (AKA GUILTY PLEASURES)

Sometimes you just need a quick fix. The following joy tools may appear different from each other, but they all have something in common: brain disconnection. They're the equivalent of sucking on a piece of hard candy to get a short, quick blood sugar bump when you're starving but currently have no access to food. Just like in that scenario, these activities can be a great temporary help until you find something better to eat but can backfire if you don't work on finding real food soon, as they can later on give you a sugar crash.

In an example directed to my fellow healthcare providers: these activities are like steroids—just like using a Medrol dose-pack. They're anti-inflammatory and quick and can treat and mask a wide variety of symptoms. But if overused, they might cause long-term issues.

Bottom line: use judiciously.

Drumroll, please. Here's my list of mind-numbing, brain-disconnecting, joy-candy activities:

1. Brainless TV or streaming.

2. Silly comedy

3. Social media

4. Silly or cute YouTube and Tik-Tok videos

5. Gastronomic pleasures (Fill in your favorite one: comfort food, sweets, wine …)

6. Escapist novels

7. Shopping

8. Computer games and game apps

9. Disconnected sex

10. Top secret guilty pleasures

BRAINLESS TV OR STREAMING

We all have done it. When I was a medical resident in training, I would return home from a long shift at the hospital. My brain had been working in high gear all day, scared of making a mistake with a patient and trying to adjust to navigating the new hospital. By the time I made it home, I was too exhausted to clean or study but too wired to sleep. I spent hours staring at the TV watching "check your brain at the door" sitcoms. Then, slowly, I would regain the ability to do something productive.

SILLY COMEDY

I'm a big believer in the healing power of laughter and hesitated before placing comedy in this group. Comedy is an art, a documented medical treatment, and for some people, a religion. At the risk of scandalizing some of my fellow physicians, I will confess that I believe so strongly in the effects of comedy rebooting the cells that I used to *prescribe it* to my patients admitted in the hospital with febrile neutropenia (a life-threatening condition due to the chemotherapy where the patient's white blood cell count is so low they get infected with their own normal flora). In my informal observations, the patients watching comedy recovered their counts much faster.

The point is that comedy spreads over a broad spectrum. The comedy I'm referring to as "silly comedy" is the lowest denominator of it. My husband calls it "fart and dick jokes." We have a rule to decide which stand-up comedian we keep watching and who we turn off, and it involves how soon into their routine they bust out profanity and how many curse words a minute they use. But, hey, no judgment here. The same comedy that David and I find distasteful can work wonders for someone else.

Another good example that comes to mind is a website that became the guilty pleasure of a group of my doctor friends. After heart-rending hospitalist shifts, they would entertain themselves laughing at pictures of overweight people at Wal-Mart bending over. Definitely not my style, but again, there's no judgment here when the goal is psychological survival.

SOCIAL MEDIA

Spending time on social media platforms such as Facebook, Instagram, and Snapchat is a good example of an activity that requires careful selection. They can become sources of pain when they're used to self-flagellate by comparing yourself to other people's apparent ideal lives and achievements. They might also bombard you with negativity when people you know decide to use these platforms for political and social justice activism. While having a cause we believe in is a wonderful way to bring passion into our lives (more on that later), I'm talking about a different use for social media platforms. That is the minimal substitute for human connection.

Nowadays, I rarely spend time on Facebook. However, eleven years ago, it saved my life. My then-husband, a jealous and controlling man, had blocked me from any social interaction, even distancing me from my family and friends. Isolated from my loved ones, I lacked any loving mirrors to help rescue me from my low self-esteem. Gathering strength to leave him started by breaking that isolation and reconnecting via Facebook with my sisters, my cousins, and my friends from high school and college—people who saw not only my defects but also my qualities and who remembered the more joyful person I was before he'd entered my life.

SILLY YOUTUBE OR TIK-TOK VIDEOS

The same scenario we discussed on comedy applies here. There's a wide spectrum of what videos you can find online, from educational experiences and inspirational speakers to complete senselessness. In the category of Mind Candy, I refer to whatever your favorite flavor of brain disconnection is. Is it cat videos? Puppies? Babies? Is it following a specific YouTuber who microwaves iPhones just for fun? The options are endless and, just like the rest of this section's activities, work better in moderation.

GASTRONOMIC PLEASURES

If your automatic response when you're under stress is overindulging on one of these pleasures by mouth, from too much wine to eating the whole cheesecake, don't put it on your list and focus on a different one. You'll probably gravitate toward this spontaneously—and cut yourself some slack about it.

Pro tip: If you are the (very normal) type of person who has trouble stopping once you start eating or drinking, I have a tip for you. Do not focus on self-control or struggle for moderation. Instead, focus on *distraction*. Like I said earlier, when we try not to think about something, we fixate on it even more. In the words of New Age writers, "What you resist, persists." And "Where focus goes, energy flows." Instead of using all your strength to fight your desire to finish the lasagna, just focus your attention on the other joy activities. The busier you are with them, the less time you'll have to obsess about food.

Here's where the Joy Diet becomes literal as I invite you to fill in your favorite way to caress your tastebuds. For some of us, it will be comfort food (Is it pasta? Bread? Desserts?) For others, it might be a go-to drink. (Is it a mug of hot cocoa? Coffee? Wine?) Notice how you feel when you think about it. If it brings a wave of guilt and self-loathing, it's not worth it. Just move on to the next activity.

ESCAPIST NOVELS

Reading is such a sacred activity in my household that I almost feel the need to apologize for including escapist reading among Mind Candy. Pat yourself on the back for being a reader in a world when readers are becoming elite.

When I refer to Mind Candy reading, I mean any literature that's directed to distract us and amuse us, not to enlighten us. Its main role is to allow us to abandon our ego and enjoy a different persona temporarily, from mass-market paperback romance to cozy mystery, to police and detective, to cowboy novels. You'll see that deeper literature that leaves you with a message and true catharsis appears in the Nutritious section. (By the way, I'm proud to claim that the romance I write is that type of nourishing reading, providing life lessons).

As I mentioned before, getting myself lost in a Mind Candy romance novel has helped me deal with some of the most difficult times of my life. And if I had any judgment left for the lowest common denominator novel that I usually don't read (steamy romance, erotica, cookie-cutter trope such as billionaire romance ...), one of my dearest patients helped me get rid of it.

This delightful lady—I'll call her Martha—shone from her perfect grooming, stylish, ladylike outfits, and her amazingly youthful appearance for her seventy years of age. She had been diagnosed with two cancers in two years (breast cancer and chronic lymphocytic leukemia). Despite those challenges, she stood out among other patients due to her sweet, sincere smile, pleasant disposition, and polite manners. One time Martha volunteered how challenging it had been to deal with her two cancer diagnoses in such a short time. I asked her what her secret to keeping her positive attitude was, and her answer surprised me.

Sweet, polite, ladylike Martha replied, "My secret is that I read a romance novel a day. The sexier, the better—my favorite ones are the hot, rough cowboy romances."

I smiled. "Well, thank God for that!"

I never looked at a "trashy" romance novel the same way.

SHOPPING

I once heard a quote from Dr. John Gray, and I never bothered to verify its source or scientific basis, but it resonated with me so much that it became one of my life mottos. The quote claimed (and I paraphrase) that the female brain derives extraordinary pleasure from shopping because it's wired for food collection. In cavemen times, while men hunted, women would be in charge of scanning trees in the woods looking for fruit or checking bushes searching for berries.

It makes sense that we women must be hardwired for shopping. Few things calm my overloaded brain more than walking down the aisles of a store placing a product in my shopping cart, which I may or may not buy in the end. Mindlessly roaming a physical store once became a form of meditation for me. Sliding hangers in long clearance racks, I would allow my racing thoughts to keep going without sticking, and eventually, they would calm down.

In some other, less joyful times in my life, roaming stores also became an exercise in imagination. Every object that called my attention broke through my self-imposed numbness and taught me something new about myself. The beach outfits, flip-flops, and sandals I could've never worn in the Chicago winter reminded me about my latent dream of moving to Florida. The cute coasters or wineglass markers I had nowhere to use reminded me of how isolated I'd become.

Just like in the food and drinks example, you might want to skip this if you have a known shopping addiction, excess credit card debt or if, like my friend Celia, you're a self-proclaimed hoarder. Just focus on the other activities and allow them to consume some of the time you previously devoted to this one.

COMPUTER GAMES AND APPS

I won't try to give up-to-date examples because the chances are that by the time I finish typing these lines, there will be a hundred new games out there. From the solitaire game that comes with most PCs to Candy Crush, from console gaming to word searching apps, there will be a wide variety of guilty pleasures to choose from. Some of them might even be educational (in which case, as you'll see, I would upgrade them to the Nutritious category).

DISCONNECTED SEX

Full disclaimer: I tend to be on the prudish side (though I'm proud to say I've come a long way over the years). So, if you feel easily scandalized when talking about sex and prefer to skip this section, I'll completely understand.

What do I mean by disconnected sex? I mean any sexual activity that is not directed to establishing a loving human connection. That includes most forms of self-pleasuring, casual sex, and any sexual-pleasure-generating activity involving someone you do not love (your legal spouse included). No judgment here.

The glory and the taboos surrounding human sexuality are too complex to try to tackle in this book. Depending on your religion, your culture, and your upbringing, you might have very strong opinions about what is acceptable sexual behavior and what is not. In my humble opinion, sex graduates to a Highly Nutritious joy-generating activity when love is involved—and someone could argue, that includes self-love. For the rest of the sexual activities that don't involve love (from using a vibrator to "hooking up"), I recommend using the same caution we discussed when approaching food, drinks, or shopping. Basically, if the activity makes you hate yourself later on, you're better off skipping it. If you consider yourself at risk of overindulging, then don't put it on your list. Instead of fighting it, focus on other activities to keep you busy and distracted.

TOP SECRET GUILTY PLEASURES

Here feel free to enter ANY activity that lifts your spirits, but you're not proud of (or you'd rather not share with people who aren't your unconditional champions). It could be that extensive stamp collection that engages you to the point of obsession. Or your love for cosplay or cross-dressing. Or that membership to that secret online club of insect worshipers. Again, no judgment here. Anything that makes us happy and doesn't hurt others deserves a place in our lives.

To illustrate this, I have a friend who is a highly successful professional woman, wife, and mother. She has a hobby that might come across as unusual and out of character for a deeply spiritual person and a feminist as she is, and she prefers not to disclose it often: she collects Barbie dolls. Not only does she collect them, she *kind of plays with them*. She displays a dozen of them on a shelf in her room, and she rearranges the display and changes their clothes and accessories regularly. At first thought, it sounds just plain crazy, but when she explains the meaning, it's easier to understand why she does it. She grew up with limited financial means. In her childhood, Barbie dolls were expensive and the one toy she dreamed of but rarely ever got. By buying new dolls for her collection, she honors her inner child and heals the powerlessness of her past. But there's more! Each doll on her display represents an archetype or aspect of her life—the mother, the lover, the businesswoman, the nurturer, the seeker of answers ... Re-arranging the dolls depending on what's going on in her life becomes a way to re-organize the pieces of her identity and her priorities.

See how the same story can seem less crazy when we shine a light of compassion over it? Well, I encourage you to shine that light of compassion over your own secret guilty pleasure, if you have one.

By the way, the friend in that story is *me*.

So if you ever had a secret pleasure that you'd rather hide from people who would judge you for it and not understand it, you're not alone. And it's okay.

EXERCISE 2

Good news! You already did it. If not, this is your chance. Go over the list of Mind Candy activities listed in this chapter, pick the activities that resonate the most strongly with you, and list them in your journal. Remember, *it has to feel good.*

For now, leave blank the other two columns, "Nutritious Activities" and "Joy Super Foods." We'll address each in the next two chapters.

5
NUTRITIOUS JOY ACTIVITIES

I CALL THESE "NUTRITIOUS AND DELICIOUS," low effort/high return activities. Think of it like getting the best bang for your buck. Unlike the previous list, these activities are not limited to plain brain disconnection (which, as we've established, is an honorable aim in itself). They also *add value to your life.*

Overall, these activities will carry a much lower risk for addiction because they come with a built-in self-limiting mechanism. Returning to our food example, it's easier to get short-circuited by junk food than healthier food—it's easier to lose control and binge on potato chips than it is binging on apple pecan salad. Furthermore, the key is also the quality of the experience they offer. In my case, I find I'm less likely to overeat if the food I'm enjoying is high quality and full of flavor. Food like that invites us to stop and savor it slowly. While tasteless food will often make us keep on eating, as we don't feel satisfied with the experience. (The first two plates of bland potato salad left me feeling something was missing. Maybe a third one will answer what that was.)

Whenever possible, I encourage you to resort to these Nutritious Joy activities first and reserve the ones on the previous list for those occasions when you just don't have the energy for anything else.

The good news? Almost every activity you selected from the previous chapter has a more nutritious alternative. I call it "your guilty pleasure's more successful cousin."

Similarly, many of the activities in this list graduate to the third list (the list of Joy Superfoods) when we add a tweak. For example, this section includes instances of art we *appreciate*. When we *perform* art (for example, we are the dancer, the painter of the picture, or the piano player instead of the spectator), art climbs even higher in the joy scale and graduates to the highest nutritional value category.

So, here's the list of Nutritious Joy activities.

1. True sensorial pleasure

2. Appreciating visual arts

3. Catharsis-inducing literature

4. Listening to music

5. Activities fostering true human connection (even if superficial)

6. Loving sex

7. Hardwired/instinctive love (pets and small babies)

8. Exercise

9. Crafts (one step below creating art)

10. Your Guilty Pleasure's more successful cousin

Let's elaborate a little on each.

TRUE SENSORIAL PLEASURE

When I refer to true sensorial pleasure, I'm talking about enjoying experiences of such quality that you're obligated to slow down and savor them. It's the difference between munching on a Snickers bar versus relishing a small piece of premium dark chocolate. It's the difference between listening to your neighbor singing in his yard versus listening to your favorite singer or band.

Notice that some forms of sensorial pleasure cross the line to the highest joy value and the point of religious experience: Those include appreciating nature, watching a sunset, and contemplating someone you love.

A little ahead, I offer an exercise to jumpstart your awareness of all the different ways you can bring sensorial pleasure into your life. This exercise will encourage you to surround yourself with beautiful objects, aromatherapy, uplifting background music, pleasant textures, delicious flavors, and appealing scents.

APPRECIATING VISUAL ART

You could call these the "visual department of sensorial pleasure." Think about your favorite form of visual arts: Painting? Sculpting? Architecture? Theater? Dance? If the previous list included watching brainless TV, this would include watching a high-quality movie with a message. If the previous list included watching a YouTube video of cute kittens, this category includes watching a well-performed YouTube video of your favorite dance, from classical ballet to hip hop.

CATHARSIS-INDUCING LITERATURE

What is catharsis? The Merriam-Webster dictionary defines catharsis as:

"Purification or purgation of the emotions (such as pity and fear) primarily through art" and "Elimination of a complex by bringing it to consciousness and affording it expression." (https://www.merriam-webster.com/dictionary/catharsis)

In other words: catharsis is to poke a sleeping monster in *indirect* ways, usually through art.

Continuing with the previous section idea: If your list of guilty pleasures included books you read for escapism, this list refers to deeper fiction books that leave you with a lesson or a message. Beyond allowing us to abandon our ego and enjoy a different persona temporarily, they induce catharsis (the release of suppressed emotions) by allowing us to ride the characters' feelings and experience their crises, resolutions, and transformations. It's a subtle difference, but it's there. Think about those books you read and never forgot. They transport you into descriptions so vivid you feel you've visited foreign places. They bring you to the edge of despair and then make your soul soar. They push you to see a situation in a new, different way that changes you forever.

My fiction is designed to do that. My novels will make the reader cry and laugh. They make you root for the characters and, in the end, leave you with an aftertaste of joy and hope.

ACTIVITIES FOSTERING TRUE HUMAN CONNECTION

Human connection is the magic touch that transforms any mundane activity into a soul-enriching one. Take the infamous social media. If instead of using Facebook to compare yourself with others, you use it to reach out to that relative you haven't seen in years, it elevates to a new level. If, instead of using it to brag about something, you use it to offer words of support to a friend in need, the experience shifts.

Take something as mindless as a video game. If you're using it to bond with a friend, a sibling, or a child instead of playing alone, the experience becomes more significant. The same applies to almost any experience we mentioned before. Whether you're watching TV or a YouTube video, if you're sharing it with someone you love and using it to foster conversation, it skyrockets on the nutritional joy scale.

LOVING SEX

This is different from the Mind Candy type of sex we addressed in the last chapter. If the goal of sex is to generate a loving connection with your partner, it immediately enhances its ability to generate joy. This type of sex has multiple known health benefits, including releasing endorphins and oxytocin that foster attachment and bonding in the couple.

Pro tip: You might argue that sex is a tall order for someone who is feeling down. When we're depressed, our libidos are the first thing to go. However, if you're fortunate enough to have a partner, I encourage you to give physical touch a try, even if it is just a make-out session or a mutual massage. There's a saying in Spanish that goes, "Eating and scratching are just about starting." Worst-case scenario, it will be a pleasant bonding activity. Best-case scenario, it will put you two in the mood for sex. And sexual appetite tends to be counterintuitive. After a while, the less sex we have, the less we crave it. Restarting some form of sexual activity will often reawaken the appetite.

HARDWIRED/INSTINCTIVE LOVE
(PETS AND SMALL BABIES)

Many of my friends and relatives who passionately love their pets would protest if they saw me placing love for a pet in a different category than love for a human. If you're lucky enough to have an animal in your life you adore, be my guest; place his or her name in the list of highest-quality-joy activities. Love is the ultimate joy generator—hands down—and you can never go wrong with it.

I'm including pets in this category, not because our love for them is of lower quality, but because *loving pets is easier than loving humans*. Pets are *not asking us to change*. And while playing with a puppy or a kitten, love flows more spontaneously, as our natural nurturing instincts tend to come out. The same goes for our instinctive love for small babies before they're old enough to defy us or give us love in return.

Playing with a dog, petting a cat, or rocking a small baby (especially one we're not responsible for) can be deeply healing. This is particularly true if the setback we're trying to bounce back from is human conflict that makes it difficult to open our hearts again—such as a fight with our spouse, recovering from divorce, or betrayal by a friend. If you don't have a loved one living in your household, I strongly recommend volunteering to take care of your friends' pets or babies.

EXERCISE AND FITNESS

I'm a physician. So, please don't get me started with all the benefits of exercise, from improving our cardiovascular health, to increasing our muscle mass, to lowering our resistance to insulin, to all those wonderful endorphin-related psychological benefits.

But in addition to being a doctor, I'm also a convert to exercise. Having grown up a nerd, I used to be a proud couch potato. Whenever I engaged in an exercise program, for example, aerobics, it was something I did with the goal of looking better and dreading it terribly.

Until the day I fell in love with bicycle riding. Riding my bike for miles and miles became another form of meditation, where I would allow my thoughts to race through my mind without dwelling on them, and, eventually, the answers I searched for would click into place. The activity filled me with so much energy. I eagerly looked forward to it every day.

Moving to a beach town where streets don't have bicycle lanes and often lack shoulders or sidewalks forced me to reduce my bike riding for safety issues. Now my favorite joy-generating exercise involves long walks along the beach. Not only does it double as my connection with nature (which bumps it to the highest-quality-joy category), but it also greatly improves my quality of life. Shortly after I started walking, I began to sleep better and experience more energy during my workday. Sometime later, during a trip to Europe with my husband, I surprised myself with my much-improved stamina, walking speed, and ability to climb hills and stairs compared to the previous year's trip.

So nowadays, I don't have to exercise discipline to ride my bike to the beach for my morning walk. I look forward so much to that ritual that I don't mind rising extra early for it.

Some friends have said the same about their gym, morning jog, or time on the elliptical machine at home. If you still don't have any form of exercise that makes you happy, then don't force yourself to choose this for your list, as it will likely not cheer you up. Later on, when you're in a better mood, I encourage you to try it, and you too might end up hooked.

CRAFTS

Do you have some manual work that you deeply enjoy? Knitting or crocheting? Building structures with Legos? Needlepoint? Puzzles? Pottery? Assembling toys?

Anything that requires repetitive manual movements can become a way of emptying the mind and, indirectly, meditation. For a while, I became obsessed with making jewelry. I loved to string beads and come up with different patterns. That also became a form of reconnecting with childhood, as I found myself almost unconsciously re-creating my mother's collection of semi-precious stone necklaces.

YOUR GUILTY PLEASURE'S MORE SUCCESSFUL COUSIN

Go over any other item you have on your "Mind Candy" list that we haven't touched yet. Can you think about a higher-quality form of it that can add value to your life?

For example, if for your secret guilty pleasure you wrote "an obsession for collecting insects," that might easily transform into a higher-quality experience if it also connects you to someone else—if you find an online club or a friend who also enjoys the topic and wants to discuss it with you. Also, time-sink phone apps rise in status when they serve to connect you with someone—like checking in with loved ones through WhatsApp. I would also place in this category apps that teach you something. My personal example of this is the app Duolingo to learn new languages.

EXERCISE 3

You got it! You already did it! If not, this is your chance. Go over the activities mentioned in this chapter, pick the ones that resonate the most strongly with you and list them in your journal, in your column of "Nutritious Activities." Remember, *it has to feel good*.

We'll address "Joy Super Foods" in the next chapter.

6
JOY SUPER FOODS

I CALL THESE "HIGHEST EFFORT/HIGHEST RETURN activities." Yes, at first glance, it would appear that these actions require more stamina and discipline, which is why I encourage you to start with the easiest ones first. But you will soon discover that after you get the hang of these activities, the good feelings they generate are so long-lasting that they keep you coming back for more. They're all different paths to the same goal: they're all activities that connect us back to our Source (God, the Divinity, or our Higher Power, in whatever way you understand them). Sometimes we'll reconnect to that divine energy by reaching for another human being or connecting with nature. Some other times it will be by reaching inside us.

This list contains options for everybody regardless of their spiritual history or lack of it. We all have different ways to connect with the Divinity. For some people, it can be following a passion. For others, it's visiting a garden or sitting quietly in silent meditation. Since the point of this book is to enhance and expand your arsenal of joy tools, I invite you to open your mind and your heart and read through all sections of this chapter. Then, you can decide what you would like to try for size and whatnot.

The Source-reconnecting activities include:

1. Unconditional love

2. Altruism (Charity, acts of random kindness, service)

3. Prayer

4. Meditation

5. Nature

6. Art and creativity

7. Learning (expanding our mind)

8. Teaching.

9. Gratitude (a category in itself)

10. Your truest passions

UNCONDITIONAL LOVE

This includes *giving* love as much as receiving it. Yes, it would be ideal that when we're feeling down, we have a pair of arms to wrap around us and a shoulder to cry on. But trust me, even if you're the person holding someone and giving *them* love, you will also experience healing.

Tell someone you love them. If expressing love aloud is difficult for you, simply wordlessly send your love. I strongly recommend the book *The Five Love Languages* by Gary Chapman to help us with that to help discover whether your loved one's favorite love language is physical touch, encouraging words, company and conversation, gifts, or acts of service.

Hug someone you care for. Cuddle up with your child. Give someone a sincere compliment. You know how to do this. You got it.

ALTRUISM

Remember the golden rule and the law of karma? Good deeds so invariably return to shower our lives with blessings that we practically should do them just for selfish reasons. We're all connected at the deepest spiritual level; when you make someone else happier, you become happier.

Altruism doesn't have to mean huge acts of sacrifice, such as following Mother Teresa's steps or donating all your money to charity. More modest acts of charity also work. This includes offering support to someone who needs it, sincerely smiling at strangers in the street, volunteering your skills to a cause, and performing acts of random kindness—God knows the world needs more kindness.

These actions are among the most effective ways to break the cycle of self-pity and recover joy. I didn't list altruism first because it takes more stamina than just exchanging love and might feel like a stretch for someone who's depressed. But that makes it all the more effective; since it implies taking *action,* it also helps improve our sense of empowerment. I encourage people to start the self-lifting process with the simpler joy activities we mentioned and then, if possible, dive right into this.

PRAYER

If you're someone who's become disappointed with organized religion over the years, I don't blame you for cringing at the word "prayer." My definition of prayer here would be: "Using *words* to approach the Divinity as you understand it." They can be pre-established words or words you're making up as you go.

Yes, we all have different ways to connect with the Divinity. For some people, it can be absorbing the beauty of nature. For some, it can be simply expressing gratitude. I'll approach those as separate items. But this method of using words (prayers) can be very soothing in a different way.

Let's take pre-established prayers. I come from a Christian Catholic background. In my adult life, I've gravitated more to a wider spirituality with less involvement in religious rituals. Still, when something brings me anxiety, repeating the words of the Lord's Prayer ("Our Father who art in heaven . . .") has a magical calming effect on me. I find myself resorting to it multiple times a day, such as when worrisome thoughts about a future cancer recurrence invade my mind, or when I have fears for my children's safety, or simply need to face tasks I dread.

There's something very healing about repeating the words that have been spoken by billions of people for millennia. The same applies to reading a favorite psalm or piece of scripture, or the Serenity Prayer ("God grant me the serenity to accept things I cannot change, courage to change the things I can, and wisdom to know the difference."). By connecting with humanity above and beyond our current small world of problems, we temporarily rise above them.

Obvious reminder: *It has to feel good.* If you have a traumatic or negative association with a particular prayer, just leave it alone.

If you happened to have grown up with religious prayers you used to derive solace from, I strongly encourage you to dust them off and bring them out again for a trial. Comforting childhood prayers can connect you again with the innocent faith required to surrender problems and trust there will be a good outcome in the end.

Or you can choose to talk to God—as you understand God. Just saying what's in your mind, asking for guidance, or even expressing a complaint, can re-open the communication channels.

MEDITATION

I haven't found the original source, but the best definition of meditation I've heard is, "If prayer is the way we talk to God, meditation is the way God talks to us."

For this book, I'll define meditation as the act of quieting the mind. This can be accomplished in many different ways, including transcendental meditation, mantra repetition, yoga, or Tai Chi.

The Internet is overflowing with so many resources and merchandise (from guided meditations to Tibetan bells) that it can become intimidating at times. But the simplest way of meditation doesn't need an app or props. It's simply relaxing in a comfortable position, breathing slowly, and trying to empty your mind.

I repeat, *trying*. It's okay not to do it perfectly.

Just like exercise, meditation was something that troubled me for years. I felt obligated to check the box of meditation because every influencer I knew claimed it was good for me. But I was skeptical about its benefits. My perfectionist side felt frustrated every time I attempted and "failed" at it—either because I couldn't slow down my mind or I relaxed so much that I fell asleep. And I still waited for the moment when I would float over my body or see the future.

My breakthrough came when I *stopped wanting a breakthrough*. Instead of striving to empty my mind, I shifted to a much more doable alternative I heard experts recommend. "Just watch the thoughts pass by, without holding on to them." Instead of trying to become an athlete of meditation, I aimed to meditate fifteen minutes at a time. It also helped to move my attempts at meditation from the evening to the morning, when I was rested and less likely to fall asleep.

And most importantly, I stopped wanting to see clouds part, skies rumble, and sudden enlightenment strike me.

Just as you wouldn't expect instant miracles when you start a new exercise program, the benefits of meditation take time. Similar to when I started exercising, the well-being that meditation generated was difficult to pinpoint at first. I noticed a little more patience with my kids, a little less pain when facing sad medical cases, the ability to bounce back from a sour mood more quickly. The difference was subtle, but enough that it kept me hooked until the results expanded. And now, a couple of years later, it's a cherished daily ritual.

NATURE

We are designed to draw energy from nature. It's practically effortless, except for breaking inertia and getting ourselves out of our chairs. Nature can also enhance another activity, doubling the return from our effort. For example, going for a run along the beach gives you the double mood-lifting effect of exercise and communion with nature. I love watching sunsets over the Indian River lagoon, which gives me a dose of nature *and* a dose of visual beauty.

Think about all the different ways you can bring nature into your life and choose the ones you would enjoy the most.

- A beach walk

- Gardening

- Watching a sunset

- Watching a moonrise or watching the stars at night

- Bringing flowers home from the store

- Visiting a park

- Hiking

- Bird watching

- Wildlife spotting

- Visiting a public garden or botanical garden
- Practicing a water sport or activity such as fishing, surfing, or sailing

ART AND CREATIVITY

Performing art is one of the highest-quality joy-generating activities. What's the difference between arts and crafts? When does a hobby of making collages and scrapbooks graduate from a craft to an art? The difference, in my opinion, is *passion*. If the activity you're performing is a pleasant, mind-relaxing task, mark it as a craft. If it makes your heart soar and gives your life meaning, then it becomes an art.

For example, take my jewelry-making phase. I loved stringing beads and creating beautiful pieces I could wear later. It was a wonderful soothing feeling, but not "a religious experience." I consider that a craft.

On the other hand, take my writing. When I write, I feel deeply connected with the creative force of God. I'm happy no matter what's happening around me or in the world. On an average writing day, I experience what I imagine a drug high must feel like. On a *good day,* I'm taking direct dictation from the Divinity. It doesn't matter if the quality of the final product meets a literary standard; for me, writing is my art.

LEARNING (EXPANDING YOUR MIND)

This may or may not resonate with you, but all my life, I've loved acquiring new knowledge. Whether that is learning to play a musical instrument, a new language, or a technique to gain joy, anything that expands my mind can elevate me above daily worries. Studying new things feels so rewarding that I've found time to squeeze it into my life despite my busy days. For example, I used to listen to French lesson CDs while I commuted to work or use the Duolingo app to practice French or Italian in waiting rooms. Another favorite of mine is taking my iPad with me to the kitchen so I can listen to self-improvement webinars while cleaning and loading the dishwasher.

Is there something you've always wanted to learn more about? Or a skill you've always wanted to master? Bringing that back into your life when you're feeling well provides you with yet another tool to resort to when you need to lift your spirits.

TEACHING

The desire to contribute to the evolution of our kind must be encrypted in our DNA. Not everyone will consider teaching a soul-expanding activity— education can be frustrating if the students are unappreciative. But every teacher or professor is nodding right now; they understand my point. Teaching might be as unpredictable as roulette or a slot machine, but when the magic happens, it's incredibly rewarding.

During medical school, I worked as a teaching assistant, leading anatomy and histology laboratory sessions. Most of the class consisted of tedious memorization of names of anatomical structures, cells, organelles, and tissues. So, to capture students' interest, I connected my class with medical scenarios and with their other courses, like physiology and biochemistry. Some of my best memories are witnessing the flash of epiphany in their eyes when a new concept clicked. They got it! And I felt as proud as if I'd single-handedly helped move civilization forward.

GRATITUDE

Gratitude deserves a category by itself, so I've expanded more on it in the section "Gratitude Journals" in Chapter 15. In more than one dark moment of my life, gratitude has been the reset button that allowed me to bounce back.

I honestly thought I had invented the concept of therapeutic gratitude myself! To encourage myself around the time of my divorce, I began a journal of the things going right in my life. The habit gave me a better perspective and significantly improved my mood. And as it usually happens when we just hang in there and keep showing up, the situations burdening me at the time unraveled themselves. I tell the full story in Chapter 15.

After that, I began recommending gratitude exercises to my patients, often to those experiencing the most difficult challenges a human being can confront. Later on, I also recommended it to the doctors in my support group for women physicians. Everyone reported a drastic improvement in their spirits.

There are two main practical ways you can apply gratitude: acute/ immediate and delayed/chronic. In the first one, I use gratitude to lift myself from acute despair. In a dark mood emergency, I quickly jot out a list of things that make me happy. Doing it feels like a reboot, forcing me to take away focus from the part of my life going wrong and pay attention to the parts going well.

The second use of gratitude is delayed or long-term and doubles with neuroplasticity. It's taking a moment to notice and appreciate when things are going right every day throughout the day and pausing for ten to fifteen seconds to savor the good feelings. I firmly believe that re-wires the brain to be more receptive to positive thoughts. To increase that capacity of noticing what's right, I strongly recommend you make it a habit to write at least five things you're grateful for at the end of each day.

YOUR TRUEST PASSIONS

Here, you fill in the blank for anything I've missed that makes your heart sing. Any activity you wrote in previous lists (even your secret guilty pleasure) can be upgraded here if it fits that criteria of making your soul soar. What is the thing that you never seem to get tired of doing? What causes do you embrace? What do you really believe in? We're looking for an uplifting feeling, rather than, for example, something you're passionately righteous *against*. So I would not include political activism. Why? Because the activities on this list must bring you more joy than frustration. Short of that, working for a cause that gives you a sense of purpose and allows you to connect to other human beings could make it here.

Besides writing, another of my biggest passions is spiritual growth and personal development. I love anything that can make me a more enlightened individual: listening to inspirational speakers, self-help books, online masterclasses … I can never get enough of them.

EXERCISE 4

You already know what I'm going to say, don't you? Go over the list of "Joy Super Foods" in this chapter, pick those that resonate the most strongly with you, and list them in your journal. Resist the temptation to write something you *should* be doing but honestly don't enjoy. Remember, *it has to feel good.* If an activity you've never done before appeals to you, it's great if you decide to try it for size, but that's different. This particular list should be full of things that come naturally to you, and you can default to them automatically when you're down.

NEXT STEPS

In the next chapter, we'll expand these lists to create our personal arsenal of joy-generating activities.

7
CREATING AN ARSENAL OF JOY AND PLEASURE

CREATING YOUR LISTS OF RESOURCES

A RE YOU READY TO EXPAND all this and apply it to your life? By this point, you hopefully have three lists of potential activities that can lift you. Now let's really milk it and focus on each sense. I got the inspiration for the sensorial pleasures portion of the list from Tony De Mello's book *A Minute of Awakening*. Here we'll combine sensorial pleasure, gratitude, and activities. I will provide some examples just to get you started. You should easily be able to get to dozens of items per heading, or hundreds, by the time you're done. Have fun doing it! Even thinking about these options feels good!

Pro tip: write this list in a journal or type it in a document on your computer you can return to in the future. Reading it again becomes a great exercise in jumpstarting gratitude.

Bonus: I had to limit this list to just a few examples to avoid going over my word count. For a much-expanded list in a PDF format, you can print or save for future use, go here to join my newsletter: https://mailchi.mp/f581a47174e1/bouncing-back

SENSE OF SMELL

Make a list of all your favorite scents in the world (**Pro Tip:** just writing them and re-reading them will be enough to lift you up. But if you want bonus points, after identifying them, get yourself a supply of them that you can enjoy a couple of times a day).

- My list starts like this:
- The invigorating scent of coffee
- The delicious scent of bread baking
- The refreshing scent of lime or lemon zest
- The sweet smell of babies
- The deep musk of rain
- The sweet and citrus lemongrass scent
- The salty scent of the ocean
- (…) (Go on. I'm sure you can extend the list to huge proportions)

SENSE OF TOUCH

The most delightful textures my fingers have touched:

- My newborns' soft baby hair
- My cat Ice's silky fur
- My favorite soft, plush blanket
- My kids' little chubby hands
- My mother's favorite silk scarf
- Exquisitely smooth velvet
- Fluffy cotton balls
- Slippery satin pajamas
- (…)

The most pleasant things I've felt against my body:

- My warm electric blanket on a cold night
- Loving arms around me (I can think of a dozen people I love who give great hugs, from my husband to my late father to my son James.)

- My silk dress robe
- That Montreal hotel's feather duvet
- A refreshing shower
- A bubble bath
- The water jets in my old jacuzzi
- (...)

My favorite sensations:

- Squeezing sand between my fingers and under my toes
- Floating in water
- Kneading dough
- Popping bubble wrap
- Squeezing bean bags
- (...)
- Add your own.

SENSE OF VISION

Make a list of all the most beautiful things you've ever seen. Mine contains items as diverse as:

- The pink sunrise over the Atlantic Ocean
- The bright orange sunset over the Indian River Lagoon
- The peaceful sleeping faces of my children when they were little
- The laugh lines around my husband's hazel eyes when he smiles
- Brightly colored fruit, such as strawberries, mangos, and oranges
- A deep blue sky on a sunny day
- The stained-glass windows of the Saint Chapelle in Paris
- (...) (Now it's your turn to add items here.)

List the most beautiful places you've visited, then describe an image you associate with them. I've been lucky to travel quite a bit, something I only started doing later in life. But you don't need fancy places, just places that have lifted your soul.

- Venice: The gorgeous buildings reflected on the canals
- The Dominican Republic, where I was born: palm trees against the turquoise ocean waters
- Downtown Chicago: the skyline against the blue sky through the train window
- Suburban Detroit in the fall: the changing colors on the leaves, yellow, orange, brown, and red
- Hawaii: the waterfalls on the Road to Hana, Maui
- Grant Park, Chicago, in the early spring: the yellow dandelions over the grass, announcing the end of the long winter
- Dubrovnik: the view of the red roofs and ocean from the top of the city wall
- Rome: the shiny cobblestone streets of in the golden hour near the Spanish steps.
- (...)

Favorite Art. This can include both famous pieces and not-so-famous pieces that you've associated with good memories.

- My mother's still-life oil paintings, packed with colorful tropical fruit.
- Rodin's *Kiss* sculpture, exuding sensuality and eroticism.
- Canova's *Eros and Psyche* statue: the winged god of Love tenderly awakening her lover Psyche with a kiss.
- Multicolor and slightly surreal Monet paintings.
- The pink, soft green, and off white façade of the Santa Maria del Fiore Church in Florence, covered with so many beautiful lace-like carvings it somehow reminds me of frosting on a cake
- (...)

Favorite Literature: (**Pro tip:** The good part about making this list is that you can always identify books worth re-reading and have them handy for a low spirits day.)

If you're an avid reader, you can even separate this point in sub-categories such as:

- Books that marked my life: *A Return to Love* (Marianne Williamson), *Homecoming* (John Bradshaw), *Getting the Love You Want* (Harville Hendrix) . . .

- Serious literature that has touched me: The Alexandria Quartet by Lawrence Durrell (especially the book *Mountolive*). Gabriel Garcia Marquez's *Ojos de Perro Azul.*

- Fun, hope-infusing books: My own novels, especially *Faith is Fearless* and *Longing for Love. Eat, Pray, Love* (Elizabeth Gilbert).

- Pure Soul candy: *Picture Imperfect* (Mary Frame), *Love Hacked* (Penny Reid)

Favorite Movies. Mine are:

- *Forrest Gump*: A homage to innocence, a fun trip through recent American history, and an inspiration for every mother of kids with special needs.

- *Pretty Woman*: A modern fairy tale and a metaphor of how we all feel wounded, flawed, and unworthy of love.

- *Dangerous Minds*: A real, inspiring story about challenging young minds and not giving up on troubled youth.

- (...)

SENSE OF HEARING

My favorite sounds in the world:

- Rain falling on a tin roof
- The babble of rivers and brooks flowing
- The soothing roar of the ocean
- The refreshing sound of my husband's laughter

- The high voices of my children as babies and young kids—especially their laughter and squeals of delight
- The birds' morning chorus
- (...)

My favorite music in the world:

Here! Go to town! I have so many and in so many different genres that I could use up all my word count here. I particularly enjoy creating playlists mixing songs that might seem very different but carry the same mood flavor: energizing, relaxing, bittersweet ... I can practically dial in the mood frequency I want to invoke to get me out of a specific negative feeling.

Some of my favorite music includes:

- Soul-shaking classical music: especially piano and strings
- Immortal oldies: 1950s music, the Beatles, Abba, Motown hits
- Latin music that makes me want to dance, from Merengue to Samba
- Instrumental contemporary music, especially piano hits
- Fun country music
- Cool, sexy bossa nova
- Energetic rock
- Relaxed and joyful reggae
- Tear-jerking romantic pop
- (...)

FAVORITE TASTES AND FLAVORS

If you associate eating with over-eating and guilt, this section might be tricky. For now, just imagine you have perfect self-control and can have just a small taste of something. Have you noticed how the most intense flavor sensation comes from the first bite or two? After that, the taste buds get numb, and the pleasure is not the same. Then, think of foods that bring you intense pleasure (my best example: dark chocolate). Think about the foods you would lay back and enjoy, rather than the type that makes you compulsively keep eating (my personal example of that: chocolate chip cookie dough). In my opinion, there are only two good reasons to eat something: 1-) It's very nutritious. 2-) It's mind-blowing tasty. You might be surprised to notice how much of what we eat doesn't make it to this cut.

Interestingly, great foods give us a double dose of enjoyment because it's not only about their flavor but also their texture. My favorites are:

- Silky dark chocolate, melting on my tongue and caressing my tastebuds
- Honey with lemon, making me wince with its tangy sweetness
- Juicy and crunchy Sea of Love sushi roll
- Deep flavor cheese, the type I can stretch for a long time because even the smallest bite is full of taste
- Addictive Honey Teddy Graham crackers (please, don't judge me).
- Ocean tasting crabcakes
- Thanksgiving sweet potato casserole, giving me a sugar high followed by a nap-seeking crash (but it's worth it!).
- (...)

EXERCISE 5: LET'S ENHANCE OLD ROUTINES

Now go over your lists and come up with two ways to enhance a routine you already have, bringing it up to the next level of enjoyment. For example, let's use your daily shower: How can you make that special? If one of the favorite smells you listed was rose scent, buy a rose-scented soap or shower gel that you can use every day instead of your plain, regular soap. If one of your favorite sensations was floating in the warm water of a bathtub, then consider replacing the shower with a bath, at least during the weekends.

Let's say that another of your routines is having a cup of coffee every morning. How can you bring that to the next level of pleasure? Treat yourself to the highest-quality coffee you can afford (and if you taste it and decide it's not worth it, it's okay to go back to your regular brand). If you enjoy the scent of coffee, take a few moments to enjoy it. Choose a day or a week to be "experimenting day" where you will try flavored coffees or add new syrups to yours (from French vanilla to hazelnut). If your list of favorite flavors includes fancy coffees, such as espresso or cappuccino, can you splurge on an espresso machine and make your morning drink superb? Are there any other ways you can make your morning coffee routine extra special, such as bringing your cup with you to the outdoors (your backyard, your front porch, the nearby park …) and having coffee while enjoying a view?

EXERCISE 6: LET'S CREATE NEW ROUTINES

Next, come up with two new uplifting activities you will commit to doing each day to cheer yourself up. One in the morning, one in the afternoon/evening. You can choose different ones each day, or you can stick to one that works. Put them on your calendar and set reminders for them on your phone. Plan to do this for the whole next month, re-evaluate how you feel, tweak the plan, and re-start it. The goal is to make this a habit as sacred as brushing your teeth.

Important: Make sure you're doing it *every day* and not only on days when you're feeling down. We want to separate "feeling down" from "reward" by rewarding ourselves consistently.

BONUS POINTS EXERCISES

While you're feeling good, prepare an arsenal of "rainy-day cheer-up activities." These are tools you will reach for when you're feeling unusually down.

Make a playlist of your favorite songs you can listen to. I have several flavors of playlists; some of them are tear-jerkers on purpose, to help me with catharsis, some are uplifting, and some are upbeat and cheerful.

Sometimes I feel that when I'm down, it's difficult to concentrate on a new book, and I find it easier to re-read one I already know I loved. Pick uplifting or distracting books you once loved and would like to re-read, or movies that made you laugh and wouldn't mind re-watching.

Make a list of ways you can pamper yourself when you're feeling stressed out or down. My list includes taking a hot bath instead of a shower, giving myself permission to indulge in a chocolate chip cookie, and pulling out an especially soothing lavender-scented shower gel.

But, again, make sure you're doing something enjoyable *every day* and not only days when you're feeling down. We don't want our brains to associate bad days with rewards and unconsciously generate bad mood days to finally earn time for ourselves.

And remember the most important step! Every time you're indulging in each of those small pleasures, pause and press the record button, savoring it for at least fifteen seconds and remind yourself, "See? I can have joy and pleasure in my life."

CONGRATS!

Great job! You just completed the first part of the program. Keep working on your exercises, and follow me to Part II. In this section, we'll put these tools into action to learn how to bounce back from adversity.

PART II:
BOUNCING BACK

JUST BY LEARNING TO READ your Thermostat and creating your Joy Menu, you're in better shape than you were before starting this book; but we don't stop here. Your list of favorite joyful activities is a collection of *tools and weapons*. In the next chapters, you'll learn how to best utilize those tools, especially in difficult times, and we'll also be adding other useful skills.

But before we dive into that, I would first like to introduce a few concepts. In the next two chapters, we'll learn about what it takes to recover from setbacks and what we can get from them.

8

WHAT HAPPENS WHEN LIFE THROWS US A CURVEBALL? THE ANATOMY OF OUR REACTIONS TO BAD NEWS

Y OU MAY BE WONDERING IF the Joy Diet is a too simplistic way to approach the human predicament. From simply having the blues to suffering from major depression, we don't need any reason, in particular, to feel down—imagine how it goes when something terrible does happen. You may also be wondering if what I propose is living in denial about the harsh realities of the world. Is it truly possible to go through life with a big smile twenty-four-seven?

Hell no.

That's unlikely to be sustainable. Life is designed to challenge us again and again—it's part of growing—and every time it does, it takes us some time to bounce back. In this chapter, we'll dissect the anatomy of a setback, and in the next one, we'll learn what it takes to recover from it.

CHALLENGES: THE SEASONING OF LIFE

What comes to your mind when you think of the words "An exquisite dessert"? I bet the idea of tasting a spoonful of sugar straight from the container doesn't come to mind (not that I haven't done it myself). Even if our tastebuds are genetically programmed to find the sweet taste appealing, the best sweets are those that throw a contrasting flavor and different textures in the mix. Dark chocolate that comes with a hint of bitter mixed with the sweet. Tangy citrus in our Key lime pie. Salty, crunchy nuts mixed into the sweet, silky brownie.

It's the same with feelings. In an ideal scenario, the lows of life teach us something and encourage us to readjust our course, but they also make the moments of joy shine even more by contrast.

THE CONCEPT OF HEDONIC ADAPTATION

If our lives consisted of constant joy and bliss, we would soon grow accustomed to them and not even perceive them; that's what "hedonic adaptation" means. Just think about so many great things in your life you have taken for granted and only deeply appreciate when you find yourself deprived of them. My simplest example? Air conditioning. When I'm inside the house, I don't even remember it's on. Yet, when I head out in the Florida summer heat and then return home, it feels glorious. And let alone if we lost power because of a hurricane! While we are sweating in the muggy, dark house, I swear a hundred times that if I can only get back A/C, I will never complain about anything in my life again.

A more serious example is my husband, David. Sometimes I'm lost in my computer, writing, and he asks for some attention. "Come make me some company over coffee," he calls me from the kitchen breakfast counter. My first, visceral reaction is of protest because it throws me off completely when I'm interrupted in the middle of an idea.

Then I remember my life before I had him—the despair during my former marriage, the loneliness of my nights after my divorce. Or worse, imagine what my life would be if I lost him. Wouldn't I give anything for the privilege of sitting at the breakfast counter chatting with him one more time? That little dose of contrast never fails to convince me to put down my laptop and rush to the kitchen, eager to enjoy him.

WHY AM I TELLING YOU ALL THIS?

Because this is the very first idea I would like to plant in your mind for this second part of the book: *It's okay to feel down at times.* Feelings of sadness and despair are a natural result of setbacks. Feelings of anger are often the impulse that propels us to make a productive change in our lives. Fear and anxiety are natural self-preserving mechanisms, and regret and guilt are part of our moral compass, making sure we don't repeat mistakes. And all those fluctuations work together, resetting us, so we appreciate the joyful moments even more.

Plastering a smile on your face is exactly the opposite of what I propose here. Instead of fighting negative feelings, we're better off embracing them, knowing that they'll usually run a self-limited course if we just hang in there.

Let's get started by studying the anatomy of bad news or a bad diagnosis: Let's talk a little bit about the grief cycle.

THE GRIEF CYCLE: NEVER UNDERESTIMATE THE POWER OF DENIAL

Once I took care of a patient with advanced breast cancer whose husband was a colleague, an internal medicine physician. For this story, I will call her Barbara and him Dr. Josh. Shortly after Barbara's diagnosis, I ran into Dr. Josh in the hospital ward, and he approached me for conversation. His exhaustion showed in his weight loss, wrinkled scrubs, and under-eye shadows.

"Elisabeth Kubler-Ross was the worst scammer in the world," he blurted with little introduction.

His abrupt statement caught me off guard, and it took me a moment to remember the scammer in question was the last century's Swedish psychiatrist who proposed the five stages of the grief cycle in 1969 and who had died about five years back.

"What do you mean?" I asked.

"Studying the grief stages in medical school was a huge waste of time. One day, my wife is stuck in anger, the next day in sadness, the next day in anger again," he vented. Then, with dropped shoulders and a dead-serious expression, he concluded, "I want to raise Elisabeth Kubler-Ross from her grave just to slap her."

His concern is one I've heard many people express before. "Grief just doesn't read the books." So I will not use this chapter for a refresher on the traditional grief cycle: denial, anger, bargaining, depression, and acceptance. They never happen in a smooth, continuous fashion anyway.

The bottom line is: when something bad happens, at first, we can't believe it. We are numb and slightly detached from the situation, and it takes a little while until what happened hits us full force. Then we'll go back and forth between anger and sadness (in my experience, favoring our favorite negative feeling), and we'll mix that with self-recrimination and attempts at undoing or fixing things in hindsight by changing our actions now (a little too late). We'll simmer in that brew for a while, and then acceptance will start emerging, first as islands in the stormy waters, later on as more solid ground.

But I do want to talk a little bit about denial because not all of it is negative. Sometimes, consciously choosing denial can have a positive impact on our managing crises.

DENIAL

Denial, the usual first reaction after a piece of bad news, can take many different forms. Some of the most common are:

1. Automatic rejection of the news. "That's impossible. Period."

2. Feeling complete numbness.

3. Detachment. The feeling that things are happening to someone else.

4. Selective blindness. Seeing something is happening in front of us and not even capturing it.

5. Selective deafness: Someone tells us something, and we just don't hear it.

6. Immediately changing the subject.

7. Inappropriate euphoria or excessive joking.

8. Forgetting that we even heard the news.

9. Projection. We hear bad news or criticism, and we immediately focus on someone else who has that problem or defect, deflecting the attention from us.

Denial has a bad rep. It evokes images of stubborn people sinking their heels in the ground, refusing to move, and images of dangerous health neglect, but it's a completely normal reaction. We've all experienced denial, from being blind to one of our defects to refusing to believe the COVID quarantine was happening. Denial is a necessary psychological stage that our wise psyches have built in for a reason. I would dare to say that it serves *three* very important purposes.

1. DENIAL AS SELF-PRESERVATION

Denial allows us to keep ourselves together without panicking when something life-threatening or identity-threatening happens.

Let's use the example of my oncology patients getting the news that something abnormal in their tests suggested cancer. If they'd deeply assimilated what was going on, they would have been too overwhelmed to coordinate their specialist visits, CT scans, and biopsies. Denial became the soothing balm that allowed them to keep going through the insane number of tests often needed to confirm a cancer diagnosis. So even when I strongly suspected the biopsy would be positive, I allowed them to hold on to the possibility of a false alarm until we received the final result. I did the same with myself when it was my turn to have a breast biopsy.

2. DENIAL AS OUR LAST RECHARGE

Denial also gives us a last taste of normality and a chance to say goodbye to our old lives, in a way, allowing us to recharge before the new journey ahead.

I'll never forget the night my mother's diagnostic process began. She had broken her arm with minimal injury, and the orthopedic doctor, knowing I was a medical student, showed me the x-rays and confided his concern that this was not a normal fracture but a pathological fracture—the result of abnormally weakened bones.

"I'm going to have the radiologist review the films to confirm the impression," he said. "But I'm pretty sure this is a bone cancer called multiple myeloma."

I did not hear the part about his certainty; all I heard was that the diagnosis was not final. The rest of that day and night, I clung to the conviction that the radiologist would refute the impression. I have a sweet memory of me that night singing and dancing in my room in a better mood than usual. I had no doubt everything would be okay. I was nineteen, full of life, and dating for the first time in my life (I was a late bloomer). I looked forward to visiting New York City in a few weeks, enjoying my first summer off from school in years. Life was good.

But the radiologist *did* concur with the diagnosis. Within twenty-four hours, I transformed from the carefree, joyful girl I'd been to the caregiver of a patient with incurable cancer. My life would never be the same

A few years later, I would look back at that night and remember it as the last moments of blissful, innocent joy before I was catapulted into adult life. And I've felt deeply grateful for having had those extra hours.

3. DENIAL AS AN UNCONSCIOUS PROCESSING TIME

But later on, I realized that despite my apparent euphoria that night, there had been a small corner of my mind, backstage, processing the doctor's words. When the official news did drop, that part of my brain took over. I did not, by far, stand in the same position as the day before. My attitude had truly evolved from, "This is ridiculous. Those kinds of things don't happen to us," to "Oh. So these kinds of things *can* happen to us."

DON'T RUSH IT

The bottom line of these stories is: don't fight denial unless it has prolonged to the point that it is threatening someone's safety. Denial is usually self-limited, and sooner than later, a deeper understanding of the implications of what is happening will reach us. It may happen in fits and starts rather than in an exact moment, so if you find islands of blissful relief in the midst of your crisis, savor them. Ignore the little voice inside you or the ones from a well-intentioned loved one who says, "You're not worrying enough. You must be in denial." *It's okay* to be in denial on and off. And it doesn't mean you'll stay in it forever. Enjoy any moment of calm you can grasp.

It's worth repeating that line: "Don't fight denial *unless it has prolonged to the point that is threatening someone's safety.*" Denial can be good and bad.

GOOD DENIAL AND BAD DENIAL

As a young medical student, I became fascinated with the difference between "repression" and "suppression." When talking about psychological defense mechanisms, repression is when our unpleasant memories or unwanted knowledge are buried out of sight, and we forget about them. I call that bad denial because it can lead to neglecting a problem. Suppression, on the other hand, is repression's wiser relative. We're still aware of the bad memories or bad situations, but we consciously decide not to focus on them. I call that good denial.

The difference might sound subtle, but it's significant. Suppression is considered healthier and a sign of maturity in the person. I believe good denial is a large component of successfully navigating life. Good things and bad things will always coexist in our lives, and we can choose into which we will pour more of our time, energy, and attention.

UTILIZING GOOD DENIAL: PANIC SERVES NO ONE

It's been documented if a crowd panics—let's say because someone yelled "fire"—more victims end up trampled to death by panicking people than die in the fire. There is a legitimate reason why, at the moment of an emergency, our minds cannot focus on assimilating how life-changing this event will be. We need all of our brain to take action.

Not to mention that there's always a chance we were worried about nothing. And the small detail that, even in the worst-case scenarios, we do not know what the future will bring, and we accomplish nothing by trying to predict it. My cousin Berto is a great example of that and an inspirational story I used to share with my patients.

MY COUSIN BERTO

My cousin Berto and his sister grew up in New York City, and perhaps because I only saw them during the summers, I eagerly looked forward to their visits. The time they spent in the DR passed like a delightful string of beach trips, mango picking, and swimming in streams—some of the best memories of my childhood.

And also some of the worst! Berto drove his sister, my sisters, and me crazy, always finding new ways to tease us and torture us—from calling us fat and ugly to blurting out disgusting statements in the middle of breakfast to ruin our appetite. His farts were legendary. Despite his relentless teasing, he brightened our lives with his unbelievable sense of humor. I loved Berto with a passion, and it's safe to say he was the older brother my sisters and I didn't have back then.

That made it the most shocking when, in his twenties, he fell ill from a rare form of meningitis that left him blind. The doctors concluded he had cryptococcal meningitis, which led to the diagnosis of AIDS.

Berto miraculously survived his severe meningitis, but the doctors warned us that his days were numbered. Back then, in the early nineties, anti-HIV drugs were still in their infancy, and AIDS was a death sentence. The whole family prepared to say goodbye to him.

But Berto refused to let the news defeat him and kept seeking other treatment options. He kept talking about going back to the gym and rebuilding his muscle mass, about getting better so he could travel the world, and about recovering his sight someday. All my relatives sighed and commented, "The poor guy is in denial." They humored him with their attention when he talked about those things, but everyone assumed he had, at best, a couple of years to live.

Berto didn't recover his sight, but he hung to life for *twenty-eight years*. In those three decades, he not only got in shape, but he also won a few bodybuilding contests. He traveled extensively—even to Egypt. He reinvented his life, getting a new career as a massage therapist, something he could excel at despite his blindness. He helped a new generation of loved ones (the children of his cousins) to grow up with a completely new perspective on life. And, yes, he outlived several of the pessimistic relatives. The miracle happened in part thanks to him enrolling himself in one clinical trial after another to get access to the newer anti-HIV medications that were still experimental. But in many cases, when one treatment had started to fail, and the next one was not yet ready, we thought again and again we would lose him. I believe he kept himself alive during those times with sheer willpower.

Thank God he was in denial all of those times when we were about to give up on him, and he found another clinical trial in which to enroll himself!

A BRIEF WORD ABOUT BARGAINING

Here's another stage of the grief cycle that often has a derogatory connotation. Bargaining entails that desperate moment when the person going through the crisis tries to negotiate a way out. "God, if you take this away from me, I will do X or stop doing Y." In the case of my cancer patients, the typical scenario was the psychological defense mechanism of "undoing." For example, a patient who smoked for decades, upon a lung cancer diagnosis, would quit smoking. Or a patient newly diagnosed with metastatic colon cancer would run to buy a juicer and an elliptical exercise machine, trying to get into a healthier lifestyle. Both intentions are great but a little too late to make a difference.

But is it really too late? It's never too late as long as we're still alive. For example, there's plenty of evidence that patients who quit smoking after their cancer diagnosis do better than those who continue to smoke. Well-handled, bargaining has fueled more than one positive, long-lasting change.

IN SUMMARY

It's absolutely normal to feel lousy after bad news or bad events (shocked, angry, sad …). Embrace rather than fight these emotions. After all, flexible and pliable objects break less easily than brittle ones.

With this rough map in mind, we'll dive into strategies to bounce back faster in the next chapters.

EXERCISE

Go back in your mind to a remote time when something bad happened to you or someone you love (something old enough that you have already moved on from it). It might be a time when someone in the family died, or perhaps a business went bankrupt, or someone lost their job. Do you remember the sequence of feelings you went through over the following weeks until you assimilated it? Can you identify a moment of shock/denial, anger, bargaining, sadness, and acceptance? If you can't pinpoint all the stages, that's okay. Close your eyes, transport yourself to that time of your life, and relive it for a few moments. Do you remember the lowest moment, when you felt at your worst? Use the four-compartment storage vessel and your Feelings Thermostat tools (Chapter 2) to clearly define what you felt at the time. I bet you were afraid at moments that you would never be able to snap out of that dragging feeling. Are you able to pinpoint a moment when something happened to make you feel better, or was it a slow return to your usual mood? If you identify positive feelings of relief or pride for overcoming that obstacle, spend at least twenty seconds savoring them.

The purpose of this exercise is to reawaken the memory of a previous recovery. In a way, you're practicing neuroplasticity when you remind yourself: "I've overcome bad events before and can do it again." Do that exercise more than once, with different memories, as long as they're events you already overcame and moved on from.

Bonus points: Journal about those times and see if you can come up with a *pattern*. What things did you do back then that helped you cheer up and turn around?

9
THE RESILIENCE MINDSET

IMAGINE LIVING WITH THE CERTAINTY that no matter what life throws at you, you can tackle it. Imagine that, even when facing terrifying challenges or deep disappointments, you retain the ability to say, "This sucks, but it's okay; I've navigated worse things before and know I can handle anything."

Well, that's how it feels to be a Bouncing-Back Ninja. I know it because *I am one*. After the mixture of interesting surprises my life has brought me (from children with special needs to cancer and everything in between), I've practiced picking myself up so many times, I've become an Olympic athlete of the sport. You can too.

In a couple of chapters, I'll share the concrete steps I follow to accomplish this. But we all know that in the middle of the darkest feelings, it can be difficult to do anything besides simmer in despair. That's why, before talking about action steps, we first need to address the mindset of resilience. This chapter will discuss the three crucial elements to cultivate to master that sport: self-compassion, perspective, and a willingness to learn from the experience.

SELF-COMPASSION

Self-compassion is the ability to cut ourselves slack. Please note this is not *self-pity*, where we slide into the role of victim, look for people to blame for what has happened, or regress to an infantile state of "if I cry, someone will come soothe me." True self-compassion means we can tell ourselves: "This sucks. I have the right to feel sad/angry/disappointed. It's going to take time to bounce back, and I'll be patient with myself."

If, like me, you're a perfectionist with a tendency to be too harsh to yourself, self-compassion also implies not beating yourself up. Yes, maybe this situation could've been prevented if you'd acted differently in the past. But maybe not. You made the best decision you could, given your limited knowledge of the situation and your emotional resources at the time.

After we extend compassion to ourselves, we're in a better position to offer compassion to others. If the setback comes from conflict with someone, I try to put myself in their shoes and truly understand their motivations. The cranky cashier who was rude to me might be having a bad day—or a hard life. The ex-husband threatening with legal action is most likely still hurt and feeling rejected after the divorce. The teenage son recriminating me for my parenting mistakes is the same little boy—and baby—who used to throw tantrums for attention. By the way, I don't know who thought about it first, but the technique of thinking about the person bothering you like a toddler does help.

PERSPECTIVE

The only situation in the world that cannot be solved is death, and even that can be healed through acceptance. If the setback you're trying to bounce back from is the loss of a loved one, I encourage you to go to Chapter 23, where I discuss healing from that kind of loss specifically.

For any other type of loss or trauma we might face, there's a mantra that I repeat to myself over and over during the darkest moments, and you're welcome to borrow or to modify to fit you better.

Are you ready to hear it?

Here it is:

"It could've been worse. Much, much worse."

The key to using this tool is to *stay in the present*. Something even more terrible could have happened. BUT IT DIDN'T. Let's be grateful for that.

To illustrate this, I will share a true story from my personal life that might earn me a reprimand for my son, who hates it when I share it. (Sweetie, I love you. Your story will help many people.) Here it goes.

THE STORY OF THE MIGHTY TINY DRIVER

One Sunday morning, I woke up to a strange noise. It sounded like a distant explosion, or maybe as if a large bookshelf had fallen forward, making everything on it crash down. Confused and clumsy with grogginess, I fumbled downstairs to check on the sleeping children, and an instinct made me walk toward the laundry room.

I stood paralyzed, gawking at a disaster zone, the laundry room filled with debris, dust still floating in the air. Through a huge hole in the drywall peeked my husband's red vintage Jaguar in the garage, also covered with debris, but my caffeine-deprived brain could not figure out what had happened.

I rushed to my son Brian's room—nine years old at the time—and found him in bed under the covers. I asked him if he knew what had happened, but he denied having a clue.

It took texting a picture to my friend Chuck, the contractor who'd gutted and remodeled our house, to solve the mystery. He immediately realized what had happened and called me back.

"Diely, someone crashed a car against that wall."

Yup. He was right.

As we learned that day, my nine-year-old son had been regularly sneaking into his stepfather's car to play inside it while we slept. He would turn the car on, spin the steering wheel, enjoy the rumbling of the engine when pushing the gas pedal, and spend a few minutes pretending to drive. But that morning, he'd pushed the gas pedal at the same time he moved the gear stick from Park to Drive. The car had propelled forward, crashed against the front wall of the garage, and gone through it. Then, scared by what he'd done, my son somehow managed to back the car out of the laundry room and return it to its original place in the garage. He dashed out of the mess and hid in his bed, pretending to sleep.

My overwhelm that day was multi-layered. The terror that my child could've gotten himself seriously hurt paralyzed me; so did the certainty that I had failed as a mother. How could I have been sleeping peacefully every night, not knowing that my kid was putting his life in danger? How could I have failed to teach this child how to behave? My boy had required support in his classroom because of a learning disability. Had I underestimated his developmental challenges? How could I leave him unattended even one minute now, not knowing what he'd do next to endanger himself?

If I could get past that layer of overwhelm, then I had the financial layer. Now we had a homeowner's insurance claim and thousands of dollars of deductible money to spend to fix the wall. Now my husband's beloved car also needed extensive repairs and bodywork (it was a miracle it hadn't been totaled) and had lost a significant portion of its market value. And, of course, there was the stress this was putting on my family relationship. I was this child's mother and would never reject him no matter what he did. But my husband (whom I'd practically just married) had no blood ties to him. Would he ever be able to forgive him for destroying his dream car? Will he resent us forever for this?

HOW I PRACTICED PERSPECTIVE THAT DAY

In the middle of all these questions and fears, I clung to a mantra, turned forced prayer of gratitude. "Thank you, God, *because it could've been worse.*" My son was alive and unharmed. He had put on the seatbelt as part of his game, and it was easy to imagine that if he hadn't, he could have hurt himself seriously. He had been playing with a car running in a closed garage for weeks; he could've killed himself with carbon monoxide inhalation—and he didn't.

Here's where perspective really kicked in: As long as he was alive and no one had been harmed, everything else was a small deal.

It could've been worse in many other ways. He could have overshot when backing the car out of the laundry room, also breaking the closed garage door. Even more! He could have crashed against one of the neighbors' cars parked on the driveway, or even worse, run over someone! The bottom half of the laundry room wall was demolished. The top half that survived contained our electrical panel. What could've happened if he had damaged it? Could my son have been electrocuted? Or at the least, could we now be facing, on top of everything, a power outage that could take weeks to fix?

After regaining that perspective, I was more able to embrace the absurdity of it all. "This will be one of the stories we'll love retelling in the future. And someday, years from now, we'll look back at this and laugh."

And we do. Now, four years later, the wall and the car are fixed, little evidence remains from that big event, and we still get a laugh out of that crazy ordeal. Furthermore, the story has enlightened many people's lives when we share it, as our friends stop to consider it and say, "Well, my kids are not the most terrible kids in the world, after all."

REELING IN A CATASTROPHIC-THINKING TENDENCY

Do you have a mind that tends to go to the worst-case scenario? Then imagining something that could've gone worse won't be difficult. Play with it! Remember, the way to keep hold of the reins is to remind yourself that IT DID NOT HAPPEN. And that's a reason to celebrate. If your brain insists on going to "But it could *still* happen in the future," I recommend doing something to break the loop of catastrophic thinking—for example, EFT/tapping (see the chapter on resources).

Call me macabre, but whatever the problem I am facing, I'm deeply aware that a hundred different worse things could've happened on top of it and didn't. This is an instance when the abundance of horrible news stories, which I normally recommend not to dwell on, comes in handy. I bet you that you can almost always find a story of someone who had it worse.

A COUPLE MORE EXAMPLES OF INTENSE PERSPECTIVE

My patient George was a wheelchair-riding medical textbook. Besides his history of metastatic lung cancer, he had emphysema (bad lungs), congestive heart failure (bad heart), diabetes (bad pancreas), chronic renal insufficiency (bad kidneys), peripheral vascular disease (bad circulation), and benign prostatic hypertrophy (bad prostate). He used to ask me to explain his blood tests one by one until he found one that was still normal.

"So, my liver function tests are still in range?" he would ask, and then would clap and cheer. "Thank God for that! At least my liver is still working!"

In a lighter example, my friend Marcia had struggled with her weight all her life, which has caused her tons of grief. Lately, whenever she finds herself in a low, for example, after gaining weight after the holidays, she tunes into a streaming show called *My 600-Pound Life*.

"Gee, that really cheers me up all the time," she says with a guilty smile. "After a while watching those poor people struggling to move, I feel much better about my 'few' extra pounds."

(Please note that practicing perspective by comparing ourselves to others must always be done with deep compassion for the other person. It's not intended to brag or gloat that we're doing better than they are but to remind us that there are others in deeper trouble than us, and we should be grateful for our lighter lot.)

WILLINGNESS TO LEARN FROM THE EXPERIENCE

The third crucial mindset needed to become a Bouncing-Back Ninja is a willingness to learn from even the most difficult experience.

Remember the story of my nine-year-old son crashing his stepfather's car? As rattling as the situation was at the time, it ended up providing me with one of the most valuable lessons of my life.

The time around the crash, I'd been overwhelmed by a hostile, competitive environment at work. I lived in constant fear that any minute my own colleagues would put me out of business. Other times I obsessed about whether I should simply resign. I spent hours without end, running potential terrible scenarios about unemployment and an uncertain financial future.

Well, the minute the shock about the car crash resolved, I arrived at a realization: I could've never, in a million years, anticipated that something like that could happen. Why did I worry about potential scenarios, which may never happen, when that couldn't protect me from surprises like this? By fretting, I accomplished nothing and wasted valuable time.

The next time something serious did happen—my breast cancer diagnosis—that concept helped me tremendously. Whenever my brain tried to fast-forward to the future and dwell in a possible future recurrence, I reminded myself, "There's no point in trying to guess the future; what actually hurts you may be what you least expected."

Guess what. Later on, I did quit my job—and it felt wonderful. I had worried so much about what to do if I saw myself unemployed and, when the moment to face it came, everything evolved smoothly. I had been suffering for nothing.

And right around that time, the world went on lockdown due to a COVID pandemic—something I could not have anticipated in a million years. Thank God I hadn't spent the past two years obsessing about my job insecurity or a potential cancer recurrence. Instead, I had *enjoyed life,* starting with traveling internationally as much as I did—something that was currently impossible.

Making a habit of extracting any possible learning from all negative experiences is so critical in navigating life that it deserves more exploration. In the next chapter, we'll explore the two main different types of problems we face and the different ways we learn from them.

EXERCISE 1 - A GAME OF PERSPECTIVE

We've talked about tons of serious issues in this book so far, so let's switch gears to something sillier. Let's make fun of catastrophic thinking. You can choose to practice this game with a friend or play it alone by writing both the question and the answer in your journal.

The game consists of coming up with a handful of caricatures of dramatic scenarios—the more ridiculous, the better—and then coming up with a way in which "it could've been worse." It should feel lighthearted and leave you thinking that your life is not as bad as you thought. If it's feeling uncomfortable at any point, it might be that the example you chose is hitting too close to home. It's okay to stop or switch to a different scenario.

Here are some examples:

Catastrophe #1: You made a bad business deal, lost all your money, and now you're homeless, living in a slum in Third World country.

Answer: It could've been worse! I could have all these problems *and,* on top of it, *also* be terminally ill, blind, or paralyzed.

Catastrophe #2: You *are* critically ill, blind, *and* paralyzed. Your wife dumped you, and your dog ran away.

Answer: Well, it could be worse. I could've been ill, blind, paralyzed, wifeless, dogless—AND also have a rash.

Catastrophe #3: A huge hurricane, a tornado, and a flood are slamming the city at the same time.

Answer: It could be worse. We could be facing a hurricane, a tornado, and a flood AND also be facing an earthquake and an alien invasion.

Remember. Make it fun!

EXERCISE 2

After finishing the exercise—and especially if you decided not to do it because it triggered negative feelings—let's wash away any residual negativity. Go back to your list of preferred joy activities and re-read it in its entirety. Then, choose one or two entries you haven't tried recently (you *have* been doing the two joy activities a day we agreed upon, right?) and practice them.

10

TWO TYPES OF PROBLEMS, TWO WAYS TO LEARN: ACUTE AND CHRONIC

B ORROWING FROM MEDICAL TERMINOLOGY, I'LL divide the challenges life throws at us into two main categories: acute and chronic. Acute problems are jolting and sudden but often time-limited, while chronic problems are issues that drag for a long time. The intensity of a chronic problem may not be as jarring (in part because we adapt to them), but they can be very draining as they become long-term. Each type of problem will require a different mindset, set of skills, and action steps to overcome them. If well managed, both acute and chronic life problems teach us something, but they do it differently. Let's explain and illustrate that.

ACUTE PROBLEMS

An acute problem is a sudden issue, setback, or obstacle we have to solve in a set amount of time. An example of an acute medical problem would be a broken bone, while an example of an acute personal problem would be heartbreak after a breakup. They are both sharply painful, relatively short-term, and need to be well healed so they don't become a chronic (long-term) problem in the future.

Acute issues usually teach us specific life skills that we can apply to similar situations in the future. My son crashing the car was an example of an acute issue teaching a specific lesson. But a simpler way to illustrate this might be the story of the first "adult" life problem I remember facing.

My first "adult" crisis

I was seventeen and still adapting to life in college. I'd been very sheltered all my life, and this was my first experience managing a budget and taking care of myself. One night out with some friends, as we exited a movie theater, I got the feeling that I was missing something. I realized I'd set my purse down on the empty movie seat next to mine and forgotten it there.

I immediately turned around to fetch it, but it was too late. Someone had taken it. I rushed to talk to the theater staff, but they just shrugged. The theater didn't have a lost-and-found department or even much of a security crew. My stomach clenched with the dreadful realization that with my purse, I had also lost my wallet. I'd lost all the cash I had to manage until my next trip home (in today's money, probably equivalent to a hundred dollars). I had also lost my college ID and library card.

For a hormonal seventeen-year-old girl, losing a purse for the first time is devastating. That night I called my mother, bawling, furious at myself for my distraction. Now I had to go through the bureaucratic drag of getting a replacement for my IDs. I had even lost my umbrella and my favorite lipstick! And the worst part, now I had no money for food or public transportation.

To my mother's credit, she restrained her overprotective tendencies and did not jump to try to solve my problem. She patiently consoled me and pointed out that since I had lost the money, *I* had to come up with a way to manage for the next week or so before my next scheduled trip home.

And then she told me the words I never forgot, "But do you know what? You learned a lesson! You will never again forget your purse inside a theater!"

Oh boy, she was *right*.

I don't remember how I managed the rest of the week. (I think I borrowed money from someone). But I clearly remember the lesson. *Forever.* Considering I was a pathologically distracted young woman, I learned to keep a close eye on my purse in public places—often keeping it hanging across my back or clutching it during the whole duration of an evening activity. I developed a sense that I call "the invisible fence." If I walk away from a restaurant table or mall bench and my purse has stayed behind, an alarm goes off inside me, and an imaginary rope pulls me back.

Yes, that day, at age seventeen, I lost some cash, a college ID, an umbrella, and my favorite lipstick. But only God knows how many times after that, I could've lost a purse containing much more and didn't, thanks to having learned that lesson.

CHRONIC PROBLEMS

Chronic problems are issues we may or may not be able to solve and extend over a long time. They tend to have periods of worsening and improvement ("exacerbations and remissions") but need constant monitoring.

Remember our analogies with the broken bone and heartbreak from the last section? An example of a chronic medical condition would be diabetes, while a chronic personal problem would be living with a spouse with Alzheimer's. In both cases, the problem will not be solved quickly but will require constant self-care and have good and bad days. Just as diabetes can eventually damage other organs if it isn't controlled, chronic life challenges can leak into other areas of our lives and spoil them if we don't take care of them.

While acute problems teach us specific skillsets, chronic problems enlighten us in a more general way. They strengthen the "resilience muscle," which allows us to become unshakable to *any* type of problem. It's difficult to see it while we're deep in the challenge, but they make our lives better in the long-term by providing us with a new philosophy of life and an increased capability of enjoying life. Like one of my favorite sayings goes, they teach us to dance in the rain instead of waiting for the storm to pass.

The best example I have of a chronic issue that has changed my life is dealing with a daughter with health issues and special needs.

MY DAUGHTER WITH SPECIAL NEEDS—A
LESSON IN UNCONDITIONAL LOVE

My beloved daughter, Irene, was the smaller twin of a fraternal (non-identical) twin pregnancy. Early on, ultrasounds revealed that she wasn't growing as fast as her twin brother. After her brother was born naturally, Irene moved into a breech position, and I had to be rushed to the OR for an emergency C-section. She required reanimation after birth.

Despite being on the low-weight side, she seemed like a perfect, beautiful baby, and we thought we'd dodged a bullet with her birth crisis. But three months down the road, when I returned to work, Irene stopped eating and stopped gaining weight. Doctors recommended a feeding tube—first, one that went in her nose, then one surgically placed on her stomach that was eventually replaced with a button. We were so distracted by her food aversion disorder—a term doctors used, which is more of a symptom than a diagnosis—that we didn't realize for a while that she was behind in her baby milestones. Her struggles with nutrition led to frequent infections and hospitalizations. And during one of those, she presented with seizures.

This pattern of febrile seizures repeated itself, and eventually, she received an official diagnosis of epilepsy. Later on, doctors diagnosed her with developmental delays and added the label of autism. Inconclusive genetic testing suggested that the combination of her seizures and autism might arise from a genetic mutation. She actually had VUS, a variance of unknown significance, in three different genes associated with severe degenerative neurological conditions, usually leading to infant death. Hopefully, that gene testing was meaningless since she just turned thirteen and is still doing fine. But imagine the terror I'd had to suppress from my worrier doctor-brain to live with the fear that my daughter could be destined to neurological decline and death.

The chronic situation with my daughter has transformed my life in several ways, but most importantly: it made me a master of unconditional love.

I had dreamed of a little girl for years (I have three sons before her, including her twin). I had so many dreams of going out to lunch together, going for mani-pedis, chatting about boys, watching girly movies. Well, the first dream to say goodbye to was lunches out. I now had a girl with a feeding tube since infancy who refused to eat. Forget about movies or chats about boys. My girl's autism delayed her speech severely and prevented her from engaging in conversation. Forget about mani-pedis or movies together. I had a little girl with developmental issues and hyperactivity who could not sit still and was prone to meltdowns in public. For a while, I felt cheated from life.

Even if chronic conditions require constant management, they can still enter remission abruptly. For me, a big turnaround moment came when she was three years old. It was one of the most stressful times of my life, deep in the middle of my divorce, and as often happens when I'm stressed out, her health issues were acting out. She presented with a seizure so long she had to be transported to the hospital by ambulance, and I was terrified that she might end up with brain damage. Or worse, that I would lose her.

I'd held her in my arms for hours while she slept deeply, as she usually did after a seizure. I just took in her beauty. Her thick, dark eyelashes resting over her soft baby cheeks. Her thick lips, that gave her face a striking, grownup beauty. Her shiny jet-black hair, disheveled. I still admired her when they transported us by stretcher to the radiology department for a brain study—I can't remember if it was a CT or an MRI of the brain. I lay on the stretcher, holding her against my chest as she slowly started moving, batted her eyelashes, opened her dark eyes, and looked up at me. I felt so deeply joyful that she was alive and waking up. If I could lose her tomorrow, at least today, I would enjoy this moment.

That afternoon, lying on the stretcher while we waited for her study, I had as much fun as if we'd been in one of my dreamed mother-daughter days out at the mall. I sang to her, and she listened attentively. I took selfies of the two of us with my phone and then showed them to her, making up games with them. Her good mood and alertness were uncommon for how she used to be after waking up from a seizure. She seemed to sense my peace and relaxed too.

She bounced back well from that episode, and so did I. I felt so grateful that she was alive and unharmed I no longer cared if she wasn't a perfectly developing child. I learned that I didn't need a "perfect daughter" to play with. I already had her. Today, nearly a decade later, she's alive, much healthier, and free of her feeding tube. Besides talking like a parrot, she has made great strides in her development, which I attribute in large part to our bond.

Learning to love my daughter one day at a time, without obsessing about the uncertainty about her future, has been exercise for my ability to be in the present moment. This skill is the foundation for most spiritual practices.

Tony Robbins says that our human brains have "a highway for anxiety and a dust path for joy." He points out that our human brains' operating system has not been updated in two million years and is still programmed to allow us to survive, scanning the jungle for whatever little thing is wrong. Well, in my opinion, a chronic problem makes us update that operating system. By having to suppress the tendency to obsess about that unresolved hanging issue, we force ourselves to learn to pay attention to *what's right* in our lives instead of what's wrong.

Beyond gifting me that valuable life skill, learning to love Irene unconditionally was a customized healing experience *for me.* I grew up with the mistaken belief that I had to be a superstar to earn my parents' approval. I was a straight-A student, a perfectly obedient child, the most polite lady in the world … Loving Irene exactly the way she is, having no attachment to what will happen in the future, made me realize that my parents love—and God's love—never needed to be earned. It has always been naturally present and unavoidable.

I don't care that my Irene will never be the famous doctor who discovers the cure for cancer. I don't mind that there is a chance she will never make it to college. I am okay with the fact that she might never give me a son-in-law or grandchildren. I just love her for what she is. That peek into what divine love might be has been one of the purest, most fulfilling experiences of my life.

GREAT JOB HANGING IN THERE!

The last three chapters were exactly that long introduction I avoided putting at the beginning of the book—because I knew I ran the risk of boring you if I didn't give you something practical first. I had to present you with the definition of those terms and lay the groundwork so you can really put your Joy Arsenal and the other tools I'll be presenting later to use. Great job hanging in there and not giving up! Now the next few chapters are the jewel of this book.

We'll only get all the benefits we discussed in this chapter if we manage our acute and chronic issues well. The rest of this book will focus on how to navigate those challenges successfully to emerge on the other side with more medals of honor than scars. The next chapter will cover the single most important action you can take to ensure that success: *processing The Event.*

EXERCISE

Grab your journal and go back in your mind. Identify one acute problem you've faced in your life and resolved successfully. Then, identify one chronic problem (present or past) that has taught you a valuable lesson. For each problem, write what lesson you learned in the process.

11
THE IMPORTANCE OF PROCESSING HURT

ONE THING I'VE LEARNED THE hard way in life is that we have to truly *process* hurt. Every time I've tried to suppress my feelings when something painful has happened to me, the pain remains latent under the surface. Often, it taints my mood negatively in a chronic way, manifesting as dissatisfaction and hopelessness until I face it. Some other times, it becomes suppressed and forgotten but resurfaces as acute pain out of the blue when triggered by something remotely similar. In severe traumatic events, not processing the acute issue can manifest later in physical symptoms and chronic pain.

The main idea I want you to get from this chapter is this: *Grief hurts, but it doesn't kill us.*

If we just hang in there for a little longer, grief will follow a natural course of peak and resolution. Eventually, we'll return to our baseline mood (the same baseline we've been working on elevating through using the tools of the Feelings Thermostat and the Joy Diet).

However, *unprocessed* guilt can continue to hurt us for the rest of our lives. It is critical that, at the moment of the traumatic or hurtful event, we give ourselves permission to feel the emotions associated with it. Natural denial will provide us with a temporary numbing mechanism, but if we numb ourselves too much or too long, we risk missing that necessary step that precipitates our healing process. To illustrate this, I'll share two examples, a silly one and a more serious one. The first one is a childhood story about dolls.

THE LIGHT EXAMPLE: MY FIRST DOLL

The Christmas I got "Dielita" or "Little Diely"—of course, I named her after myself—is one of my earliest conscious memories. I was three years old.

I studied her in awe for a long while before unboxing her. She was the most beautiful thing I'd seen in my life. Blonde hair, blue painted eyes, a little red, white, and blue dress, with tiny fake-pearl buttons. I fell in love for the first time in my life, and it was love at first sight. From that moment, she became more than my doll: she turned into my best friend and soulmate. It almost didn't matter that she wasn't really alive, and her soul and personality were my inventions.

I have no recollection of taking her out of the box. My memory jumps to me sitting on the black vinyl seats of my father's old white Datsun as we traveled to a Christmas celebration at my grandmother's house. I held Dielita in my arms, enjoying the smell of a new doll in her plastic hair and feeling the love flowing from me to her. Hours ago, I didn't know she existed, yet now I could not imagine my life without her.

That image, sitting in the car's backseat with my sisters, holding Dielita against my chest on our way to my beloved grandmother's house, is my earliest vivid memory of bliss and innocence before the fall from paradise. I was safe, I was loved, and I lived in a wonderful world. I had received this beautiful present in a magical way. I still had no concept of the poverty around us. I still hadn't noticed the barefoot, naked kids in the Dominican streets begging for money. Still, my mother had not announced—like she did a few Christmases later—that my sisters and I should not bring our Christmas toys to our grandmother's house because they could make our cousins, whose parents were at a financial disadvantage, feel bad about their more humble presents.

Fast-forward a few years. With birthdays and Christmases passing by, my doll collection expanded, yet Dielita always held a special place in my heart. Like it always happens to dolls, she got scuffed and dirty, and her hair became a beehive mess. She lost her original nice clothes and I kept dressing her in homemade doll clothes made out of socks and leftover fabric from my grandmother's sewing projects. She miraculously escaped the day my little sister Nathalie used a pen to scribble over the faces of several of my dolls. She eventually lost her right arm, and sometime later, she lost one leg, too (the occupational risks of having a younger sister). Among all this, I never stopped loving Dielita.

Then, when I was eight, my father got a new job, and we had to relocate to a larger city. The week we were packing for the move, my mother announced, "We should not bring trash. Any doll that has a pen-scribbled face or missing parts should be thrown away and not brought to the new house."

"No!" I protested fiercely, with the innocent self-confidence of a child. "If all my dolls don't come with me to the new house, I am not moving!"

My parents and older sister found it hilarious. They laughed at my dramatic tone and re-told the story to every single person they encountered (they actually did it for years and years to come). They probably didn't realize how ashamed I felt.

That embarrassment did it. I stopped fighting and surrendered all my broken and scratched dolls, Dielita included. They never made it to the trashcan. My babysitter took them to the poor, country neighborhood where she lived, where even smudge-faced and limbless dolls were a coveted privilege. I fabricated a story in my mind that having donated those dolls to poorer kids was a nice, Christian thing to do and that "made me feel better about it." It didn't. But I wrapped myself in a blanket of strength and kept going. Needless to say, I hated the new city with all my heart and never felt I belonged there.

For the next twenty-seven years, a thick layer of numbness rested on top of that memory, hiding the true extent of the pain that caused me. I remembered the events clearly (my family wouldn't let me forget it as they continued to retell the story like "something cute" in every family gathering). Every time someone repeated the story, faint waves of sadness wanted to re-emerge in me, but I kept them under control.

Until that night, journaling on the couch, near my thirty-fifth birthday. I'd just started therapy, and my counselor assigned me "debriefing" journaling exercises. I had to write everything I remembered from different stages of childhood, and I experimented with writing sometimes in English and sometimes in Spanish to access the memories through different filters. One night I was journaling in English and arrived at the memory of my family moving to the new city. Maybe the language switch made something click differently in my brain. When I had to translate *Dielita* to English,

I translated it as *Little Diely,* and the sentence read: "And then we moved away, and I had to leave Little Diely behind."

A dam broke. I cried and sobbed for hours. I had to cover my mouth not to scream and wake up the kids sleeping in the nearby rooms. It was true: by leaving Dielita behind, the happiest stage of my childhood had been torn away from me. I'd been uprooted from the neighbors and friends I loved and brought to a city I hated. But most importantly, that had been the birth of "the pleaser"—the "perfect little girl" who suppressed her wishes, her needs, and her dreams to comply with the expectations others had of her. It was also the birth of hopelessness and powerlessness and the birth of self-shame.

That discovery left me raw and tender for weeks. But something wonderful came from there: I had finally drained that pool of repressed, sad feelings I'd blocked from my consciousness.

The interesting part is that, as you can see, *the memory* wasn't blocked. I did remember the events. I had blocked *the feelings* associated with that memory. Reconnecting with those emotions and releasing them gave me amazing relief and propelled my healing process dramatically. And as it always happens, the moment you shine a light over a memory and bring it from unconsciousness to consciousness, ninety percent of its power over you disappears.

Could all that have been prevented? Could I have saved myself twenty-eight years of low-grade depression and not fighting for what I wanted, if back then, I'd had a chance to properly grieve and say goodbye to my dolls? I'll never know. But uncovering that process set me on a path of self-healing that eventually led to my freeing myself from an oppressive marriage once I realized I didn't have to be the "good little girl" who always tried to please her parents and do what others considered right.

By the way, about five years after that journaling episode, now in a whole new life and happily married to my husband David, I found Dielita on eBay. Of course, it's not the exact same doll (this one has both legs and arms), but it must be the same type. Even if I couldn't remember the brand name or toymaker, the second I saw it on my iPad screen, my heart jumped, and my inner child yelled inside me, "That's her! We found her!" I bought her and re-dressed her as a symbol of healing my wounded inner child, and that has been one of the most healing experiences of my life. That was how my doll collection started.

THE NOT-SO-LIGHT REPRESSED MEMORY: THE CONTINUATION OF MY CAREER BURNOUT STORY

Remember my introductory story about how I had decided to become the best freaking oncologist in the world's history? Here's another chapter.

When I was on chemotherapy, my nausea proved difficult to treat even with the strongest medications. Out of ideas, I decided to try hypnosis for it and report back to my patients on whether it helped.

I admit I expected a hypnotherapist to look like a circus illusionist or a fortune-teller holding a crystal ball. Instead, I encountered an impeccably dressed, bright woman with a contagiously peaceful personality. Lori, a former NASA software engineer who'd studied hypnotherapy as a second career, loved the idea of working with an oncologist and wanted to show me the wide range of services she could offer my patients. After a quite successful session to help mitigate my chemo side effects, she offered me some complimentary sessions and got me hooked.

In a subsequent meeting, I mentioned my conflicted feelings about the career of oncology, and Lori offered hypnotherapy to help me sort them out. I was skeptical at first. I'd been in therapy around the time of my divorce and binged on self-help books, so I considered myself an expert on sorting out my feelings. But I accepted.

One day, while digging into my dissatisfaction with oncology, I surprised Lori and myself by bursting into tears. Sobbing, I declared, "I have a morgue inside my psyche."

"A morgue?" Lori asked with her characteristic calm.

Between sobs, I nodded. "It's a room filled with corpses, skeletons, and ashes. The remains of all those patients I was unable to help."

And then I lost it.

I cried with so much violence, sobs rocked my body and pierced my throat. An avalanche of names and faces I had blocked from my memory flooded me—all the oncology patients who had died under my care—heartbreaking cases I had been unable to grieve because I needed to keep going and take care of the next patient without having a chance to mourn.

From Kelly, that uninsured nineteen-year-old girl who'd died from acute lymphoma and neutropenia from the chemo to Jerry, my beloved seventy-five-year old painter who lived four years, double his lung cancer prognosis, yet that still had not been enough for all the canvases he wanted to fill with his art. I hadn't forgotten any of those patients. But I had disconnected the memories from any feelings until that day.

Somehow, Lori was able to pull me out of my despair and out of hypnosis. I went home, grabbed my journal, and spent the afternoon writing a letter saying goodbye to patients I hadn't had a chance to have closure with. More than a hundred painful cases I'd seen over fifteen years of practice returned to mind. I'd forgotten many of the names, yet I still remembered their stories with excruciating detail. I cried for each of them, asked for their forgiveness for having been unable to help them more, and one by one transferred their ashes to the new imaginary sacred burial place where someday I would build a mausoleum for them—a new career.

I noticed a dramatic, almost instantaneous improvement. The next day I arrived at work feeling as light as if I'd put down hundreds of urns of ashes I'd been carrying. I felt as if every heartbreaking case I saw that day was a little easier to treat because I was dealing with *one* patient—the one in front of me at the time—and not with the collection of fifteen previous years of sad stories. If I ever have any chance to work with cancer patients again, it will be thanks to that grieving exercise.

The conclusion of this story is that if it happened to me—the self-proclaimed expert on self-help and self-care—it can happen to anybody. When a significant loss occurs in our lives, we have to give ourselves permission to stop, assimilate the event, and feel the feelings associated with it.

Whether your tendency is to suppress sadness, anger, or fear, if you don't acknowledge your feelings when they arise, they will remain latent inside you. They will spoil our joy baseline and likely resurface, making things worse the next time you face a challenge.

CONCLUSION: GET THE TRASH OUT EVERY DAY

Trust me—it's much easier to prevent a huge mess from occurring than clean it up once it has happened. I strongly encourage you to work with a counselor on any unprocessed grief from the past. Take my word for it; doing so will boost your capacity to feel joy.

But even if you don't feel ready (or a good fit) for therapy, acknowledging emotions regularly and giving yourself time to process setbacks will leave you with a cleaner slate for the future. Sometimes it's as easy as checking your Mood Thermostat regularly, noticing when someone has hurt you, and journaling about it to vent it out.

I could fill a book with examples where numbing my feelings resulted in years of pain until I finally embraced them. Many of those examples revolve around hurts from my first marriage. Healing from each one of those scenes took several sessions, reconnecting with different families of feelings: sadness, anger, fear, and regrets.

By the way, it may sound that going back to relive sad moments is masochistic and pointless, but I promise you it's worth it. Every time I uncovered one of those painful memories and allowed myself to feel the suppressed emotions, I felt as if my soul had been washed clean. It might take a few days, but each time you'll feel strengthened and much closer to a life of joy and purpose.

Furthermore, learning to take the trash out every day has been incredibly helpful in my current, joyful marriage. Whenever my husband does something that upsets me, I don't ignore it. I journal about it immediately and process it. Then I decide if I need to talk to him about it or not (surprisingly, more often than not, just putting it on paper makes me see it from a different perspective, and I no longer feel a need to complain). That strategy helps me prevent grudges from accumulating, and years into the relationship, I can give testimony that it really works.

DO WE REALLY, REALLY, REALLY HAVE TO DO THIS?

If the idea of revisiting past setbacks to heal them makes you cringe, I encourage you to visit the "Troubleshooting" section and read the subchapter, "Digging into Feelings Is Just Not My Thing." Otherwise, I hope this chapter has solidified that important point I needed to emphasize before jumping onto the step-by-step guide to bouncing back: Allowing ourselves to feel a little pain now can save us a ton of pain later. We sometimes avoid negative feelings because we think we'll get stuck in them and won't be able to get out, but that fear is as chuckle-worthy as when our parents used to tell us, "Don't make grimaces. Your face will be stuck like that." On the contrary, processing feelings is the fastest route to moving on. The following exercise is designed to help you practice the skills of processing feelings and then letting go.

EXERCISES (AND TWO NEW TOOLS)

The following exercises are among the most useful tools you will get from this book. Try them and decide if either or both can become a routine in your life.

1. **The Truth Serum.**
   This exercise is a more thorough version of checking the Mood Thermostat.

   Step 1: Choose one current problem or one event in your recent life that is bothering you. For example, your husband left a mess in the bathroom earlier, or yesterday a colleague gave you a backhanded compliment.

   Step 2: On a page of your journal, write the heading: "The truth, the whole truth, and nothing but the truth." (Or simply "TTTWTANBTT").

   Step 3: Write *exactly* what is in your mind about that. Don't censor anything. Are you angry? Sad? Scared? Annoyed? Take it to the next level. Dig for the *real* issues hiding under the obvious ones. Are you upset about this mess in the bathroom? Or is it about the five-hundred previous messes you had to clean before? Are you annoyed with your colleague's comment? Or did it remind you of the putdowns your older sister used when she talked to you?

You decide how long you want to keep going (I recommend doing it until you have nothing else to say). Yes, you're allowed to cuss. The only rule is: Whatever you write has to be *completely true*. No politeness allowed.

No excuses. No judgment to yourself. Also, no blaming someone else for something that deep inside you know is your responsibility.

I guarantee that just doing this—bringing suppressed issues to awareness and admitting they exist—will feel like a relief and will start weakening the effect of what's bothering you. But if you do end up unburying something upsetting from the past, the following exercise is an excellent way to clear it. (You can also do the following exercise on its own.). I call it the Closure Letter.

2. **The pro-exercise:** The Closure Letter.
   Here is where I am obligated to give you a legal warning: If you are dealing with severe trauma—such as sexual assault, childhood abuse, or severe PTSD—or if you're dealing with suicidal thoughts, it might be unsafe to try to do this on your own. In those cases, I strongly recommend that you contact a professional. If you're uncertain, try this first with what you consider a minor hurt.

   Step 1: Pick one unhappy memory from the past. It can be a disappointment about something you wanted to achieve and didn't, or resentment against an ex, or even losing someone. Anything that, when you think about it, you can feel negative feelings that hint you haven't resolved it.

   Step 2: Imagine you're writing a letter of complaint (except it's a letter we don't intend to ever send). The receiver of the letter might be someone (alive or dead) related to that negative memory whom you haven't forgiven yet. Or it could be *you* if you're having trouble forgiving yourself. Alternatively, you might choose to write the letter to God, the Universe, or life. In that letter, you'll explain why you're unhappy about the outcome of that situation and will vent why you think you were cheated of your rights.

   Step 3: This step will likely start spontaneously, but if not, do it consciously: make sure you devote some spotlight to *all* types of negative feelings. How does this situation make you sad? How does it make you angry? Did it cause you shame? Guilt? Is the memory mixed with fear, either because the event in question scared you or because you're currently afraid you won't be able to move on with your life? What regrets do you have about it? What do you wish would have been different?

Depending on the seriousness of the topic you choose, this can take you just fifteen minutes or can take you weeks—taking breaks when emotions are getting overwhelming and restarting later. Make sure you drain the abscess. Don't rush it. As you work on each feeling, you will be able to sense whether you're done or if there is more that still needs to be squeezed before moving to the next feeling. You will know you're done when you run out of tears, or you feel exhaustion mixed with peace inside you.

Step 4: Very important. Then, when you're done with those negative feelings, end the exercise with *gratitude*. Thank the person or situation in question for whatever lesson you learned from it. Even the worst ex gave you some moments of happiness in the past. Even the most evil boss taught you something. Even traumatic experiences made you a stronger person, more able now to help others in the same situation. Enumerate all the good things you got from that time of your life—in the case of exes, children count—and then give thanks. Give thanks for anything you learned from the situation and end with two sentences. "And now I let it go. I'm ready to move on with my life."

Step 5 (Optional): Depending on how charged that session was, sometimes it is helpful to have a symbolic gesture of letting go. For example, you can take the pages you just wrote and burn them. Or you can rip them into many small pieces and spread them in the ocean.

You can repeat that process as many times as you like for any bad memories you have.

Bonus points: Make sure to savor any feeling of peace, relief, or joy that may arise from that session by hitting the record button and dwelling on the pleasant feelings for fifteen to twenty seconds. You'll be retraining your brain to be better able to let go and feel peace in the future.

12
A STEP-BY-STEP APPROACH TO BOUNCING BACK IN ONE-TWO-THREE

IF YOU SKIPPED THE BEGINNING of the book and are starting here, welcome! I recommend that you take one step back and read at least Part I and the previous couple of chapters; they will lay the groundwork for the strategies presented here.

Finally! We get to apply everything in a concrete and practical way. In this chapter, I share the step-by-step process I follow to bounce back from setbacks. It is designed for *acute* problems, but they also help in exacerbations and relapses of chronic issues—in other words, every time your chronic problems previously under control start haunting you again. I came up with the steps in retrospect after using this process mostly unconsciously for years. You're welcome to tweak them and adapt them to yourself. I have no doubt that by practicing them, you can also become a Bouncing-Back Ninja.

And now, let's get working!

I jokingly call this process "Bouncing back in one-two-three." This process includes seven steps but can be outlined in three statements that capture the essence of the plan. These are: 1-This sucks, 2-Pick yourself up, 3-What's the lesson?

Just like the steps of the grief cycle are not contiguous and jump out of order, these steps I'm about to share will be fluid and often simultaneous. You might find yourself wanting to backtrack to one of the steps after you've moved on. It's okay. Play it by ear. But I recommend that you keep the first and last step in that order. The foundation to all future healing is making sure that you don't skip step one (assimilating what is going on and processing the feelings). The last step (finding solutions) will definitely be better if we first made sure to return to a place of peace instead of pain.

Are you ready? Here we go. The seven steps are:

1. Breathing through the waves

2. Grounding yourself in the storm

3. Engaging in mindless (not brainless) activity

4. Remembering perspective and gratitude

5. Finding the lessons to be learned

6. Lifting your spirits while staying in the now

7. Looking for solutions

STEP 1: BREATHING THROUGH THE WAVES (AKA: THIS SUCKS—AND IT'S OKAY)

One of the biggest breakthroughs of my life came one Monday afternoon in the middle of PMS. I'd just finished a hard day working in oncology, facing the usual heartbreaking stories, and had to rush home to drive my children to karate and ballet. I felt exhausted, but it would be hours until I could finally change out of my work clothes and rest. Then, I opened my email and found a bickering message from my ex-husband and his wife, criticizing my parenting and threatening legal action about disagreements I can't even remember.

Disheartened, I grabbed my journal and vented about how overwhelming it was to juggle work and single motherhood while also dodging the attacks of a resentful ex. Sometimes I wondered if I could keep going.

Then, as I wrote, I detached myself from the situation for a moment and realized something: Very little had changed from a week ago when I felt gleeful. I still had the same job, the same after-school activities, and the same grumpy ex. The only new details were this *one email* and PMS amplifying my feelings like a megaphone. I imagined I watched the waves

D Pichardo-Johansson, MD

of PMS hormones—and anxiety and hurt—rise and fall in my bloodstream, and an idea came to mind. "This hurts—but it won't kill me."

I'd been there before many times. I knew that if I just hung in there, in a few hours (or a day or two), those hurtful words in that email would stop having power. Even more, in a few days, my hormones would level off, and everything would look smaller. I just breathed through those imaginary waves rising and crashing over my soul and kept going.

SELF-PRESERVATION, PAIN, AND SUFFERING

If you've ever faced physical pain, for example, breathing through labor contractions or waiting for pain medication to kick in after surgery, you know what I mean here. The real pain is less if we don't add our panic and self-beating thoughts to it. Whoever said it was right: pain may be unavoidable, but suffering is optional.

A large amount of our suffering comes from the oldest parts of our brain, designed to overreact and light up like Las Vegas neon signs whenever we feel pain. That's because uninterrupted *physical* pain would kill us. But here's some news for that old brain: *emotional* pain won't. Just remembering that and allowing the more mature parts of our brain to take charge can take away the edge of the panic and make it easier to step into our emotions without avoiding them.

FEELING THE FEELINGS IS THE WAY TO PROCESS HURT

That simple shift has helped me tremendously over the years. Whenever I'm in the middle of an overwhelming situation or have just received bad news, I give myself permission to feel the sadness, anger, fear, or regrets knowing, "This sucks, but it will not be forever. This hurt, but it will be getting better soon."

The time after receiving bad news is a moment to welcome any feelings. Those mean that the initial denial is giving in, and therefore they mean progress. This is the moment to cry if needed, to scream and cuss against the pillow, to curl into a small ball in bed throwing a pity party. Heck, sometimes I would recommend making yourself cry (or scream) if you have trouble expressing feelings (see the chapter on troubleshooting "I feel completely numb.")

Let the feelings flow. The better job you do at allowing those feelings now, the less likely something will return to hurt you in the future. And no, I promise you, you won't get stuck in the bad feelings, unable ever to come out. You know yourself better than anyone. If you tend to get stuck in sadness or negative feelings, set a subjective deadline to stop feeling sorry for yourself and work toward moving on. But until then, cut yourself slack and embrace your right to sulk.

Find a soothing mantra and stick to it. Many people I know like the phrase, "This, too, shall pass." I prefer a quote my mother loved that, later on, I found out belonged to Thomas Fuller: "It's always darkest before the dawn." I repeat that during down moments while also repeating to myself, "Just hang in there." And very, very important: this is the moment to truly apply the mindset of *self-compassion*, cutting yourself slack for anything you believe you could've done to prevent this (see Chapter 9, on the mindset of bouncing back).

STEP 2: GROUNDING YOURSELF IN THE STORM. (AKA: WHAT DO YOU KNOW FOR REAL?)

Starting with this step, everything gets fluid, and you'll probably be doing all these simultaneously. You may need to pick up some "mindless-not-brainless activity" to organize your thoughts before getting to this step. But I decided to present it first because often, when we've just received bad news, it can feel we are standing on quicksand instead of solid ground, or that the world is spinning around us and we can't make sense of anything. To ground yourself and regain a small sense of direction, you need to find an anchor. For many lucky people, that anchor is religion, spirituality, or faith. But often, in our darkest moments, even that solace seems to evade us. In those cases, I recommend anchoring to your truest values and passions.

To illustrate this, I will share one of the stories that inspired me to write this book.

MY FRIEND AND HER SON

We were in the middle of the Florida lockdown during the COVID-19 pandemic when my friend Marcia called me, panicking. The bank had called her home reporting suspicious activity on her husband's credit card.

She confronted her sixteen-year-old son, John, and—to his credit—he confessed immediately. He had taken his stepfather's credit card, withdrawn cash, and got an Uber to visit a friend across town in the middle of the night. And by the way, they also withdrew money to buy pot—illegal in Florida, even for adults. And what's more, this was not the first time he'd done it.

As Marcia wept and sobbed through the video chat call—the quarantine didn't allow us to meet in person—I experienced déjà vu from the time my nine-year-old had crashed my husband's car. I could fully understand her multi-layered horror. The disappointment about her son's misbehavior piled on top of the terror that he could've hurt himself while she slept—and all that piled on top of feeling torn because her son had done something that hurt her husband.

"My son is a thief," she whispered, her face streamed with tears. "John betrayed his stepfather and me. He's going to end up in jail, ruining his life, and it's all my fault. I failed to shape his moral character."

I disagreed; I had witnessed Marcia do everything humanly possible to help her son for months. She had him working with both a psychiatrist and a therapist to tackle the anxiety, depression, and self-esteem issues she suspected were the root of his pot use. She drug-tested him regularly. She had him on a spiritual program at home that included daily prayer and meditation. Right before the pandemic, she'd mentioned how proud she was that he'd made his school football team. And more recently, she had expressed how pleased she felt because he was doing very well with distance learning and helping with chores in the house. From the outside, I could see better than she could that John was *not* a criminal, but a teenager making bad choices and learning from trial and error. But there was nothing I could say to soothe her. And the most frustrating thing, through video chat I couldn't even hug her or offer any physical support.

A while into the conversation, Marcia fell into a loop where every other sentence she said consisted of "I don't know." She began to doubt that anything positive her son had accomplished in his recovery had been but a con artist's scam. She doubted everything she ever did in her parenting. She was starting to lose faith.

"I don't know what to do," she repeated again and again, around sobs, as her breathing escalated. "John says he's sorry, but I don't know—I can't trust him anymore. His father, my ex, wants to send him away to military school—but I don't know. My husband is furious and said we should kick him out of the house, and I'm sure he didn't mean it—but I don't know." She approached a panic attack. "And if any other person in the world would've stolen money from my husband under my own roof, I would kick them out myself! I'm so angry with him—But I love him."

"That's it!" Desperate to find something to anchor her, I grasped that last sentence. "That is *one* thing you *do* know, right? You do love John."

"Of course I do." Marcia shot me a baffled look like I was crazy to doubt that.

"So, let's just hold on to that for now," I said. "That's your footing. That is the one thing you do know for sure, and you can use it to guide your next step."

Marcia's expression brightened. "Well, you are right. That is *one* thing I can trust is true, no matter what." Her breathing slowed and her trembling tapered down. "So, kicking him out of the house is out. Let's start with that."

Over the next few minutes, I envisioned the world around Marcia had stopped spinning. A moment before, she was drowning in river rapids, and now, she'd found a rope to hold on to. She still faced a precarious situation, surrounded by turbulent waters, but the currents weren't dragging her anymore. And the small edge of stability that gave her allowed her to think more clearly about her next step.

Yes. At that moment, she didn't know if John was just a teenager testing boundaries or a potential criminal. She didn't know if he was a young boy having a setback on his way to recovery or a pathological liar manipulating her. She didn't know if the pot was just a phase or the beginning of even more serious addictions that would eventually swallow his life. She had no idea what the future would bring.

But she knew she loved him.

That little piece of truth became what Marcia held on to for those early decisions that eventually would become a plan of action. She loved John, so kicking him out of the house was not an option. She loved him and would miss him too much, so sending him away to military school was not an option. She loved him, so she would never give up on him.

Marcia continued her program of drug-testing, therapy, and spiritual work with John. Shortly after the incident, he got a job to pay back his stepfather for the money he took, and that has done wonders for his self-esteem and sense of responsibility—while keeping him busy and less likely to get in trouble. He continues helping with chores and keeping his curfews. Marcia knows this is not the end of the battle, but as of the writing of these lines, John continues to blossom each day. And she still holds on to her anchor of love, to never give up on him.

YOUR TURN

The same way Marcia grounded herself on the value of her love for her son, you can find footing on the things that matter the most to you. What do you consider absolute truths? What are your deepest values? What axioms rule your life? If you don't know the answer to those questions, I invite you to take a moment to look into it. Later in this chapter, I offer a tool to clarify your core values.

STEP 3: ENGAGING IN MINDLESS (NOT BRAINLESS) ACTIVITY

When denial about a setback eases off, and pain hits us, the drumming, negative thoughts can become obsessive. As you probably know, it's useless to try to stop thinking about something. The shortest way to a solution is to think about something else or unplug the brain altogether.

Remember the Joy Menu and the list of brain candy? When we have no energy for anything else, we'll feel tempted to numb ourselves, resorting to our favorite guilty pleasures and brain-disconnecting activities—whether that's watching reality TV or resorting to alcohol. However, as we've established, processing the feelings is vital at this stage. I strongly recommend avoiding those numbing activities and only using them for an emergency—meaning when you don't have the energy for anything else and are scared of being left alone with dark thoughts. Needless to say, if you're having serious self-harming thoughts, you need to reach out and get help.

An alternative to brain disconnection I recommend instead for this stage is mindless activity. This is performing simple, productive tasks we can do automatically and don't require too much concentration. Organize a drawer you've been avoiding. Pick up your favorite craft again—from needlepoint to jewelry-making. Clean the kitchen. Weed the garden. Tackle that pile of junk mail accumulating at your door. If you feel the need to resort to brain disconnection because of overwhelming thoughts, consider combining it with mindless activity. Instead of just lying in bed with your iPad, binging on Netflix, bring your iPad to the laundry room and fold clothes while watching the shows. Instead of having a glass of wine on your couch, feeling sorry for yourself, have it while organizing your closet.

There is a reason behind the cliché character who cleans whenever she's nervous. Productive activity definitely helps us organize our thoughts. Doing something can also be soothing because it sends the brain the message that we're not powerless.

STEP 4: REMEMBERING PERSPECTIVE AND GRATITUDE. (AKA: IT COULD'VE BEEN WORSE)

Sometimes, when one of my boys is having a "teenager drama moment," I snap my fingers, point at them, and say, "Quick! Five reasons to be grateful. Go!" I also do it to myself. Often, when I find myself caught up in a loop of negative feelings, I grab my journal and jot a list of everything I am thankful for, and that helps me instantly. Gratitude is such a powerful tool that I devoted a section to it in "Other Tools and Resources."

But what happens when we're deep in the middle of a problem so big that our minds refuse to focus on anything but catastrophic thinking? In those situations, I reframe my perspective. I remind myself that things could've always gone even worse.

THE MILLION WAYS SOMETHING COULD'VE GONE WORSE

Do you remember the perspective exercise in Chapter 9? No matter how terrible the situation you're facing, you could always find a way in which it could've been worse. Even if that is "This could have happened, AND I could be dead too, unable to work on damage control." The phrase "It could've been worse" has become a mantra for me both during acute events and to manage the chronic, subtler negative feelings of guilt that come from my perfectionism.

A humorous example: one day, my oldest son, Alex, accused me of not caring for him because I'd missed most of his high school varsity football games. During his junior year, my excuse was an exhausting job and four children, including twins with special needs who could not sit still at a game. During his senior year, going through cancer treatment, I thought I was justified in skipping them. Too late, I realized my son saw it as a way of me choosing his siblings above him, and he held grudges about it.

Despite my heartfelt attempts to apologize and reassure him about my love, he continued to use the topic against me (by then, probably more as a way of teenager manipulation than true hurt). My guilt flared, and I self-flagellated for a while.

Then one day, I decided instead to tell my son and myself a more humorous story. "Well, it could've been worse," I said. "I could've missed your game not because I was working, taking care of your siblings, or recovering from chemo—but because I was a crack/meth/heroin addict passed out on the couch." On other occasions, I would smile and tell him. "Well, it could've been worse. Instead of a mother who missed your game, you could've had a mother who murdered you and threw you into a lake when you were five."

This exercise on perspective is particularly useful when the things bothering us are less significant day-to-day obstacles, but it also works for serious events. It's a reminder that much of what we call problems would be called just an annoying inconvenience by someone else who had a harder lot than us.

And the most important part: after you've identified ways in which your problem could've gone worse, take a moment to express gratitude because it didn't.

STEP 5: FINDING THE LESSONS TO BE LEARNED

I heard Oprah say once—probably quoting someone else—that we'll be stuck in a situation until we have learned the lesson it came to teach us. I also loved a quote by Michael Beckwith that says when we're trapped in a problem, we should ask ourselves, "Which quality do I need to give birth to in order to survive if this situation were to remain the same forever?" Throughout my life, I've confirmed the truth of both quotes.

LIFE: THE BEST PLOT EVER WRITTEN

Here's another way to see this point: The parts of fiction writing I enjoy the most are plotting and character development. When I'm inspired, incredibly vivid characters jump into my mind and beg me to give them life. Scenes pour into my brain faster than I can type them, and more often than not, the characters dictate what's going to happen to them in a way quite comparable to free will—I'm the writer and planning what's going to happen, but the characters ultimately have a right to veto my plans. Truly, writing fiction has given me a small peek into the mind of God as He balances free will and predestination in our lives. (If you prefer to replace the word God with "Universe," "life," "your higher self," or any other term, feel free to do it.)

And I must say, God is a *darn amazing plotter.* In an expertly crafted novel, when the reader arrives at the story's climax, all the pieces should start falling into place. "Of course, this person is the murderer! I should've known it when the detective found that clue halfway through the book!" "Oh! Now I understand why the author dropped that hint earlier." More often than not, when I look back on my life, I see those pieces falling into place. Even moments that felt devastating at the time were the propelling force that made me arrive at the next stage of my life. The dream job I didn't get saved me from working for a company that eventually went bankrupt. The love story that never happened allowed me to be free when the right person did show up. The seemingly senseless disappointment allowed me to touch bottom, so I would make a drastic decision to change my circumstances.

We won't always perceive it when we're in the middle of heartbreak, but later on, through hindsight, we'll see the learning or life skill we're acquiring. Just like me losing my purse and my umbrella at age seventeen saved me from losing much more in the future by making me more alert.

I strongly encourage journaling during heartbreak, when our original wounds from infancy are the closest to the surface they'll ever be. Pay attention to the voices in your head and find similarities to other heartbreak moments you've had in the past.

A simple example. One time, after launching a book and having a disappointing number of sales, I found myself journaling a repetition of my deepest childhood wounds. "I'm invisible. Nobody likes me. I'm the nerd the popular kids don't want to play with." Unburying those old beliefs, bringing them from the subconscious to awareness, is already the beginning of healing them—especially if we can recall a particular incident of our childhoods that triggered them. Chapter 15 lists a few tools for changing negative beliefs, including tapping (EFT), and affirmations.

If journaling doesn't appeal to you at the time, try prayer or meditation. Ask yourself, "What is the message from this situation?" and then listen. If an idea comes to mind, jot it out right away.

This book was born from a collection of such moments.

STEP 6: LIFTING OUR SPIRITS WHILE STAYING IN THE NOW. (AKA: WAITING FOR THE GREEN DYE TO WASH OUT)

I loved living in Chicago those years I trained at Northwestern University Medical Center. (If it hadn't been for my inability to tolerate the winters, I might still be living there.) One of the things that made me smile about Chicago was how enthusiastically the city celebrates St Patrick's Day. Not satisfied with changing the lights on top of the main skyscrapers to green, every year, the city dyes the Chicago River green by pouring into it twenty-five pounds of eco-friendly, vegetable-based dye.

I read somewhere that the process is only intended to last for the St. Patricks' Day parade and washes away in under a day. However, I remember seeing residues of the green dye still present for a couple of days later. It always amazed me how nature could take care of restoring things to normal.

Why am I telling you this? A few months ago, I was feeling down after a clash with a loved one. As I took a walk on the beach the following day, as part of my "Mindless activity" routine, an idea sparked in my brain. "Of course, it's normal that I still feel down: all those neurotransmitters (brain chemicals) of sadness, anger, and disappointment were poured into my bloodstream just yesterday. But just like the green dye from the Chicago River, if I hang in there, they will wash away in the next day or two." I was right. Ever since, the image of the residues of green dye is something I return to when I'm down. "It's okay. Be patient. Those neurotransmitters of sadness will unavoidably be washed away."

The best way to allow for that natural process of us returning to our joy baseline might sound like a cliché, but it's true: it is to take it one moment at a time while staying in the now—evading our minds' tendencies to jump to the future and worry about things that haven't happened yet. How do we do that? Great news! You already have the main tools; the biggest one is that list of joy-generating activities you made in Chapter 3. In this step, you get to put it into practice.

PICKING YOURSELF UP

It's worth repeating this warning: Don't wait until something bad happens to treat yourself; do it regularly. You don't want your unconscious mind to associate feeling down with getting a reward and generate bad days just to force you to give yourself some love. (Trust me, our unconscious can be very sneaky and even cause real physical illnesses).

With that warning out of the way, let's return to Step 6. This is the time to pull out your joy-generating list and dive into it. If you allowed the earlier part of this plan to evolve and gave yourself permission to feel the negative feelings without numbing them, you can claim the reward for a job well done and pamper yourself. Treat yourself like you were recovering from an illness. Get your favorite food, or use your favorite scented shower gel. Indulge in your favorite activity, whether that is curling in bed with a book or going dancing.

But here's what's different from the usual self-pampering: I want you to keep checking your Feelings Thermostat regularly, adjusting the activities as needed. For example, if you're scoring high in the fear/anxiety compartment, focus on the most relaxing items on the list, such as soothing music or a bubble bath, or exercise to burn the cortisol. If you score high in sadness, choose the activities that energize you, such as upbeat music or watching shows that make you laugh. If you score high in anger, go for that item you know returns you to balance: from patting puppies and kittens to practicing kickboxing.

The more you practice joy items from your list, the better you'll become at pinpointing which activities help for the different types of feelings. I compare it to tuning up a musical instrument using a tuning fork.

STEP 7: NOW LET'S LOOK FOR SOLUTIONS

Sometimes we can't postpone it; we have to take immediate action for our own safety or someone else's—like removing ourselves from danger. Often, the adrenaline of the acute event and the temporary protection of denial will help us make excellent quick, temporary decisions that will later surprise us with their soundness.

Short of that, I strongly recommend delaying decisions until we have taken the previous steps. Only when we've restored a minimum level of peace will we be in the best place to approach solutions. Like Albert Einstein has been quoted saying, "We cannot find a solution from the same mentality that created the problem."

DETERMINING YOUR VALUES

To find a solution, we must first anchor ourselves in something we know for sure it's true. I used love as an example in Step 2, but your anchor can be a variety of things as long as it fits one simple criterion: It's one of your *values*.

If you haven't had a chance to define your values, this is a good moment to do it, and then you can always return to that list when you need to make serious decisions or when you're in moments of heartbreak. Your values are lighthouses that will guide you during dark, foggy nights. Not only do they help you make decisions in alignment with your higher self, but they also infuse any moment of life with an additional level of flavor. When our actions align with our values, unpleasant work becomes more bearable, and pleasant tasks become deeply satisfying.

Many authors have published guides on how to discover your values. My favorite method (probably because I'm a writer) is to read lists of value words and mark the words that resonate with me. Then, I narrow my list to those four or five words that encompass others and leave me energized just by reading them.

Here is one list of over two-hundred value words and a great method to get started, from business coach and author Scott Jeffrey: https://scottjeffrey.com/core-values-list/

If you're having trouble defining your values, be patient with yourself. First, I recommend making this list in a moment when you're feeling in high spirits, so you can tap on those values that represent the best version of yourself. Second, it might be easier to start by listing *your passions* and letting them inspire you to remember your values. Are you passionate about a cause? About art? About someone? Your passions will also assist any decision process by becoming deal breakers: any decision in contradiction with one of your values is automatically ruled out. Also, any decision that would cause you to give up one of your passions must be questioned. After you define your values, I challenge you even further: rank them in order of importance to you.

As an example, here's my list of highest values:

1. Love

2. Joy

3. Integrity

4. Spiritual Growth

5. Service

And here's my list of passions:

1. My family (husband and children)

2. Writing

3. Helping others be happier and better versions of themselves

4. Learning

5. Music

AN EXAMPLE OF USING YOUR VALUES IN DECISION MAKING

I had to put all my values and passions to work to make a decision not too long ago. I'd just given my ninety-day notice at my job as an oncologist when the COVID-19 pandemic exploded. My husband became deeply worried that I might catch the virus while working at the hospital. Knowing that my history of receiving chemotherapy potentially put me at higher risk, he begged me to stop going to work and not to complete the remainder of my notice time.

"Why would you care what your bosses think about you if you're leaving anyway?" he insisted. "And this might be life or death for you; it's justified."

It was tempting. I didn't have a great relationship with that company and dreaded going to work. I hesitated not because I feared letting my employer down, but rather my patients and my staff. They were still assimilating that I was leaving in a few weeks. If I left prematurely, many of my patients would not have a chance to say a proper goodbye before my departure, which, in all honesty, didn't seem likely to happen anyway since all non-urgent medical visits were on hold for the time being.

What a dilemma! My patients needed me—but so did my family. Schools were closed, the kids needed supervision for distance learning, and my babysitter didn't feel comfortable leaving her house, given her own health risk factors for COVID. I realized that any service I could offer my patients would be limited, as I constantly worried about my risk of infection and the uncertainty of who would take care of my children.

In the end, the collective weight of my strongest values and passions (love for my husband, my family, and restoring the joy that job was robbing from me) won, but to honor my values of integrity and service, I didn't just stop showing up, as my husband had suggested. Instead, I presented a formal request from my employer to exonerate the last six weeks of my notice, and they agreed.

CREATING AN INTENTION

Once you have your list of values and passions handy, take a moment to create an intention for what you want to accomplish as you search for a solution. In other words, even before you figure out what you want and how you will get there, ask yourself: How do you want to *feel* once the issue has been solved?

This is critical. Sometimes we focus so much on finding a solution we forget that the whole purpose of it is restoring our peace and well-being. For example, if you just lost your job, you might feel tempted to take the first job offer you find to solve the problem of being unemployed. However, if you first take a moment to define *why* you want a job, you'll soon see that not all jobs apply. Perhaps you're looking for a new job because you love your family and want to provide for them—however, taking a job that requires a long commute to another city will cause you to rarely ever see them. Perhaps the deep reason you want a job is restoring the sense of abundance in your life—yet that particular employer, despite paying well, robs you of that feeling due to their competitive, scarcity mentality. The clearer you are in outlining what your ideal situation is, the more likely you'll identify the right opportunity.

DEFINING A GOAL

Once you know how you want to feel, then you can translate that into something concrete.

Continuing with the example about finding a new job, your goal could read, "A job located within fifteen miles of my address, that pays X amount of money and gives me X benefits and X amount of time off."

If your intention was meant to be vague—just focusing on how you want to feel and letting that be your compass—your goal is meant to be *specific*. Make it measurable, define clear requirements, and give it a time frame or deadline. You can always course-correct as you go if you notice that you're walking away from the feelings stated in your intention.

Here are some pro tips to help you better express your goal and intention.

Positive terms, always: Most goal-achieving experts will tell you to make sure you write your intention and your goal in *positive terms*. Our unconscious minds have a limited understanding of the word "no," "not," and "don't." If you create a goal that reads, "A romantic partner that doesn't cheat on me," your mind will immediately focus on cheating and fuel any related old emotional scars. Instead, write, "A romantic partner who is faithful and loyal."

Season it: Do you remember that list of values? Your list of passions? Sprinkle them in your intention and your goal. Use energizing and joy-infusing words that make your heart skip a beat. For your intention, not only say, "Restoring peace in my marriage." Say, "Re-infusing my marriage with love, passion, mutual respect, admiration, joyful friendship, and harmony." Do you notice the difference in the energy when you add a few meaningful words?

Present tense: Experts will also tell you to express your goals and intentions in present terms. If you express it as something "you want," "wish," or "hope for," the simple "want" words tend to emphasize the feeling of lack. Furthermore, many personal development experts recommend starting your intentions, goals, and any affirmations you might create around them with the words "I am," reportedly the most powerful words in any language. Continuing with the example above, instead of saying, "I want to infuse my marriage with love and passion," you say, "I am infusing my marriage with love and passion." Did you feel the difference?

IN SUMMARY

I hope all those tools and definitions I presented earlier are starting to make sense. To summarize this chapter, it's critical not to rush whenever you're faced with an acute setback. Take your time processing what happened and feeling the emotions. Avoid numbing yourself, and ease yourself back into life through productive activity. Then, only after you've returned to a better inner place, search for solutions. And always remember our best solutions come from the higher version of ourselves. To get there, we want to restore our joy and anchor in our values.

This chapter doesn't have an exercise because it's mostly an integration of what we've learned until now. You decide which of the tools you need to practice more—from practicing reading your Thermostat to writing a list of values for the first time.

WRAPPING IT UP

Congratulations! By finishing this chapter, you just earned the certificate of completion for the basic course in happiness and bouncing back. The remainder of this book will give you an *advanced degree*. Why? Because dealing with a chronic issue is a much more challenging situation than dealing with an acute problem and requires a different approach and a larger set of skills. In the next chapter, we'll dive into that.

13

THE RECIPE TO MANAGE CHRONIC CHALLENGES. "IT'S NOT A SPRINT; IT'S A MARATHON."

CUTE BLOWS CAN CAUSE INTENSE pain, but they're usually short-term. Dealing with a *chronic* life challenge—a long-term problem that's always hanging over your head in ebbs and flows—can be much more draining in the long run.

But like we mentioned earlier, chronic challenges can be the most transformative experiences in our lives, propelling us into great growth and much deeper happiness in the future. They push us to upgrade the operating system from the original two-million-year-old mode of survival (paying attention to anything wrong and reacting to it) into a mode of gratitude (learning to actively notice the other parts of our life that are going right). That's why I list them as part of the "advanced course" in joy. They're like resistance added to the workout to push our resilience muscles to the next level.

If we need to be Bouncing-Back Ninjas to deal with acute problems, then to deal with chronic issues, we need to become spiritual masters. They require much more of something that we only touched on when talking about acute issues: *surrendering*.

SURRENDERING VERSUS GIVING UP

Often, the belief that surrendering means giving up can prevent us from finding peace in the middle of a chronic trial. We can even feel like we're betraying ourselves if we accept an undesirable situation. I've experienced it myself.

When doctors diagnosed my daughter with autism, developmental delays, and a possible chronic neurologic condition, I found myself trapped in the middle of two options. The first option was to say, "I refuse to give up on my daughter. I'm going to work harder than any parent has ever worked, and I'm going to prove the doctors wrong." The second option was to say, "I need to love and accept my daughter exactly as she is, and never condition my love to what she can do or achieve."

Don't both options sound similarly convincing? Which one could I choose?

The answer is both. Dealing with a chronic challenge, from a child with special needs to an incurable illness, requires the mental athleticism of holding both ideas in our mind at once: "Yes, I will never give up my hope, and I will continue to work to improve this situation." And "I accept this situation exactly as it is and surrender completely to the probability that it might never improve."

Ouch. The last option sounds painful and difficult, right? However, it is the base we return to periodically to make strides in our work. To achieve that, we need to embrace three ingredients.

THE RECIPE FOR LIVING WITH A CHRONIC ISSUE

While my recipe for bouncing back from the acute setbacks included seven components, this one has only three (though, granted, each of them is more complex). I call them ingredients instead of steps because they're simultaneous, more a lifestyle rather than a one-time change. We'll be bringing those ingredients in different variations when we touch different versions of life challenges. Are you ready?

Those components are:

1. Radical acceptance

2. Constant mood vigilance

3. Staying in the moment

LET'S START WITH WHAT WE KNOW: MOOD VIGILANCE

The entire first section of this book was devoted to discussing mood vigilance. To refresh your memory, what I mean by this is:

1. Reconnecting with your feelings: Learning to read your own Mood Thermostat and practicing speaking the truth and nothing but the truth to yourself.

2. Creating a Joy Menu you can use daily to raise your baseline and also resort to when you need to lift your spirits.

3. Expanding your Joy Menu by tweaking old routines and introducing new ones.

4. Applying the Mindset Triad to setbacks: Self-compassion, perspective, and willingness to learn from the experience.

Now let's expand on the new concepts.

RADICAL ACCEPTANCE

I first learned about dialectical behavioral therapy (DBT) from listening to Oprah interview Lady Gaga, and it has fascinated me ever since. Radical acceptance is the concept of ceasing to fight reality. It's when you reach the state of "Yes, this sucks. Let's just roll with it." While this mental state may take some time to achieve, it instantly brings relief from pain and struggle.

There is literal magic about accepting what is while keeping our sight on what we want to be. It's the magic of releasing resistance. To phrase it in New Age language, to achieve any goal, we need to be detached from the outcome. If we're too attached to the outcome, we block the flow of our own energy and handicap the results.

Releasing resistance through acceptance immediately starts changing things. The tricky part? We can't fake it. We cannot say, "I'll pretend to accept the situation, so then I can get what I want." We truly have to arrive at that point when we say, "This sucks, but I embrace it."

Now let's talk about the art of staying in the moment. As usual, I'll illustrate it with a story, the story of that time when I finally learned that skill through practice.

STAYING IN THE MOMENT

I'd never considered myself a brave person or someone with a high pain tolerance. So when I decided to have bilateral mastectomies instead of a simple lumpectomy for breast cancer, I just wanted to get it over with soon. However, issues with my surgeon's schedule meant the surgery had to be postponed three weeks, leaving me twenty-one days of obsessive worry.

I've been so healthy all my life that the only major surgery I'd ever had had been the emergency C-section for my daughter. Mixed with the exhaustion of dealing with newborn twins, the memories of my surgical wound pain haunted me. And now I was supposed to have that done *twice*, one wound on each side of my chest. And the mastectomies were only half of it! At the same time, I would be having an axillary lymph node sampling surgery and placement of plastic tissue expanders in preparation for future reconstruction. Survivor friends had scared me with tales about how incredibly painful it was having those "two rocks stretching your ribcage." Oh, and by the way, that was only the beginning. The minute I had healed completely from the surgery, I had to start chemotherapy. Then, even when all this was over, I would spend the rest of my life fearing a recurrence or metastasis.

The worst part: I still had *three extra weeks* to worry about that grim future before I could even attempt to do something about it.

What can you do when you know that the future holds for you something that will be extremely painful? What can you do when your life is on hold, waiting for something that's just the preamble for more challenges, and every minute feels like an eternity?

You have to surrender, acknowledge you have no control and hope for the best. You have to force yourself to be present in the *now*.

If it was true that some of the most painful and defeating moments of my life were waiting for me, didn't it make sense to use this time to gather all the strength I could? This was the time of life to push the breaks instead of the gas pedal. To savor this moment, storing it up, so I could reach for solace when/if times got harder.

So every day, I rode my bike the three blocks from my house to the beach and walked barefoot on the sand for a couple of miles, savoring the salt-scented ocean breeze in my face. Wasn't it likely that I'd be longing for those beach walks when I had to spend my days lying in a chair, healing from surgery? I made sure to spend fun time with my husband and children every day. Wasn't it likely that I'd miss their laughter the weeks I'd be recovering and joy had to be postponed?

And just like that, one day after the other, savoring and giving thanks for my life each day, the three weeks went by.

Guess what? The surgery ended up being much less painful than I anticipated. The recovery was incredibly fast, and the one big hiccup—the second surprise cancer—was something I could've never predicted anyway, so there was no point in anticipating. Yet, the one thing I was worried about didn't happen.

PLEASE HELP! I CAN'T STAY IN THE MOMENT!

I can almost hear you protest, saying, "That sounds very nice *in theory*. But it's extremely hard to do in practice!" Or perhaps, "Well, you must be super-strong or something, But *I* am not that enlightened." Take a deep breath and bear with me.

Yes, I admit staying in the present moment is a discipline that needs to be practiced for a while before we become skilled in it. To help you jumpstart that skill, I have a great practical tool. I call it the Time Machine approach. I'll briefly introduce it here, but I'll talk more about it in the next chapter.

So, what is the Time Machine tool? I've discovered that one of the best ways to ground myself in the present moment is, paradoxically, to take a brief conscious trip into the past or the future. But this is a *planned* trip, as opposed to an involuntary one.

At that time, when I was waiting for my surgery, I imagined forty years had gone by, I had survived cancer, and I was now an elderly lady—a widow—at the end of my life, looking back. Wouldn't I do anything to go back to this time of my life and spend even one more hour here? When my wonderful husband was still alive, healthy, and loving. When my kids were still minors under my roof? When my twins were still children?

The purpose of this mental trip is to break hedonic adaptation and remind yourself of everything good in your life. If the concept still feels blurry in your mind, don't worry. I elaborate on it and offer a few more examples in the next chapter.

WAIT, ARE YOU ASKING ME TO BE IN DENIAL?

You may also be wondering if living in the moment while ignoring the possibility of a grim future is equivalent to being in denial. For that, I want to remind you of the difference between healthy and unhealthy denial.

Remember that *repression* is the unconscious defense mechanism when we block painful memories or worries from our conscious mind by forgetting about them. (They're not really forgotten; they're still latent and threaten to resurface and flare up any minute). *Suppression*, on the other hand, goes one step further. It's the psychological mechanism of defense that allows us to *consciously* block worrisome thoughts from our minds. We haven't forgotten about the painful issues, but we choose not to focus on them and instead focus on other, more pleasant, things.

Well, that's my favorite definition of enlightenment, borrowed from Buddhism: living one day at a time, focusing on the present moment.

Living in the now not only relieves pain and anxiety in the moment, but it ensures we preserve energy and are in a much better position later on to face whatever we encounter. You may be worried about nothing and just wasting precious time brooding. Like in the case of my surgery, when I was pleasantly surprised about how relatively painless my recovery was. The greatest example of that is my cousin Berto (read his story in Chapter 8). If, after his AIDS diagnosis, he would've allowed himself to fall into depression and anticipate suffering, he would've missed some of the best experiences of his life over the next twenty-eight years.

THE WORST TYPE OF CHRONIC ISSUE: CHRONIC DISSATISFACTION

Chronic dissatisfaction (what I call low-grade misery) is an insidious variant of chronic challenges, and I consider it the worst form of unhappiness. In this situation, our life circumstances are not bad enough for us to call for a change, but not good enough to leave us fulfilled. The situation might be less painful than "real problems," but "real problems" at least have a component of excitement and peaks of adrenaline that keep us going. Normally people just resign themselves to chronic dissatisfaction saying, "If it's not broken, don't fix it." And "Better is the enemy of good."

Being stuck in a mediocre situation can be soul-draining until we finally reach a point of breakdown. And what if we never reach that breakdown and waste our lives living half-heartedly?

For example, sometimes, I have to offer support to a friend who is heartbroken after a breakup or divorce, and I sincerely feel happy for them. Deciding to end a painful relationship at least comes with hope for the future. It is so much better than the alternative I see in other people I know: being chronically miserable with a spouse they dislike and not having the guts to move on. I was once in that situation during my first marriage, so it hurts me to see people trapped in the same way.

In another example, for years, my uncle Don complained about his job of twenty years. He dreaded it but stuck to it because if he gutted it out for ten more years, he could get a lifetime pension. It seemed worth it, but it meant postponing his joy of living a decade more.

Sometimes, these situations teach us to be happy with whatever we have; sometimes, they bring the message that we need to break our glass ceiling and seek something better. How can we differentiate? It's an ethical dilemma of self-love and desire for self-improvement, against having realistic expectations about life's ups and downs.

Untangling this ethical dilemma would take another entire book, but I will share what worked for me in the past.

1. **Use the Truth Serum exercise.**

   Speak the truth, the whole truth, and nothing but the truth. Even if, in the end, you make a conscious decision not to do anything about it, allow yourself to fully feel your dissatisfaction without sugarcoating it. Journal about your frustration with that job you're not happy about. Write a letter you never intend to send, explaining to your spouse why you're unhappy. In my experience, more than half the time, putting what's bothering us in writing deflates its power and feels like a big relief. It allows me to have a more realistic view of the situation and even identify ways to improve it.

2. **Determine exactly what your ideal situation would be.**

   This is something I recommend for every situation when you acknowledge that you're in a place where you don't want to be. It starts by deciding *exactly where you want to be*—by clarifying what you want.

Begin by capitalizing on your negative state instead of fighting it. Write down all the reasons why you're unhappy with your current situation.

- "I'm unhappy with my husband because he never shows me affection anymore."
- "I'm unhappy with my job because it's not intellectually stimulating."
- "I'm unhappy living in Michigan because the winters are too harsh."

After finishing the rant comes the fun part. Take every single item on the list, upend it, and convert it into what you really want.

- "I want a husband who's loving and affectionate."
- "I want to do a job that's intellectually stimulating."
- "I want to live in a place where it is summer all year long."

Then, have fun; get into the specifics. Write exactly how much money you want to make in that new job, the benefits you want, the vacation you want. Write exactly what your ideal partner is like. This exercise will shift your perspective from what is going wrong to your desired goal or outcome. That alone will make you feel better. Your unconscious mind will work in high gear, picking up conversations, cues, and pieces of information that can lead you to your next job opportunity (and yes, even noticing those rare occasions when your spouse does behave right).

Once you're clear in what you want, often miracles happen: Either you'll find the strength to leave your situation, or you'll discover a way to change it so it better matches your dreams.

3. **Now comes the fine print.**
   After you write exactly what you want, you need to write another list: Who do I need to become to create/win/deserve this life? In essence,

create a moral inventory to acknowledge what you need to change in yourself.

Did you say you want a more affectionate husband? Then perhaps you need to become more affectionate yourself, someone who pays attention to the gestures of affection and *lets them in.*

Did you say you want a more intellectually stimulating job? Then maybe you need to prepare your brain with challenging activities, instead of mindless TV.

Sometimes, the necessary change will be to improve our self-esteem enough to see more clearly that we're in the wrong place.

4. **Don't rush yourself to make a decision.**

Ask yourself why you are having so much trouble deciding to leave your current situation. Run the decision by your highest values. You may discover that two of your values are competing for dominance and determining which of the two is more important may be the tiebreaker. For example, when I struggled with the decision to leave my dreaded oncology job, the values of self-love and health-preservation competed with the values of love for my family and duty to provide for my children. I became unstuck when I realized that the psychological pain I endured was contagious and affected my family. It also helped to admit that some of what stopped me from quitting—pride and desire for success and status—were not really my values but society's. They, therefore, weighed less than the love for my family and myself.

5. **Live by the recipe for dealing with chronic issues we discussed earlier.**

Radically accept what you cannot change, such as the fact that your boss is who he is and will never turn into someone else. Live in the now, and build mood-lifting activities throughout your life, especially gratitude for what's going right. Usually, when we focus on what's right in our life and lift our spirits, we start repelling negative people and situations. And often, we find that the solution presents itself.

IN SUMMARY

Chronic challenges require more long-term stamina than acute problems, but when well managed, they present us with some of our greatest growth opportunities. To manage them, we must consistently fill our own cup and find the balance between surrendering to what is without giving up on what can be.

Since we deal with chronic challenges for the long haul, we need a wide arsenal of coping tools that we can rotate and always keep fresh. In the next section of the book, I'll offer you more tools and resources and will help you troubleshoot the most common roadblocks.

PART III:
ADDITIONAL TOOLS, RESOURCES, AND TROUBLESHOOTING TECHNIQUES

NOW, LET'S REINFORCE YOUR ARSENAL and troubleshoot moments when you may feel stuck. Whenever possible, I will credit original sources in case you want to learn more. However, some of these tools and concepts are part of collective consciousness and can't be attributed to a specific author. If I have missed a primary source, please email me with it, and I'll be happy to correct that in a future edition of the book.

I will start with one tool I created—but it's a sure bet someone else somewhere in the world thought about it before.

14

MY FAVORITE TOOL TO PRACTICE SAVORING THE PRESENT: THE TIME MACHINE APPROACH

WHAT IF WE HAD THE ability to travel to the future, to a time in our lives when our current problem is already solved, and gain solace, knowing everything will work out in the end?

Wait, you might say, what if things *didn't* work out and we don't like what we find? What if we learn something awful? Well, the most likely scenario we might encounter during a trip to the future would be a mixture of those two extremes.

The Time Machine tool is an antidote against hedonic adaptation. By taking imaginary trips to the future or the past and imagining (or remembering) a life very different from the one we're currently living, we enhance the present moment.

You've probably taken time trips to the past before, to remember good times. But have you ever remembered vividly a past time when your health, finances, or love life were doing much worse? Didn't you feel suddenly grateful when you returned to the present? I certainly have done that many times. For example, by remembering my previous, unhealthy marriage, I deeply appreciate my current, happy one.

But what I'm proposing here is a little more elaborate than a reminiscence or a daydream. Allow me to explain it with a couple of examples.

TRAVELING TO THE FUTURE

A few months ago, I talked to my younger sister, Nathalie, during the peak of the COVID-19 quarantine.

Nathalie had taken the first month and a half of lockdowns and curfews with the strength of a warrior, but now cabin fever haunted her. With no signs of the situation resolving anytime soon, she was running out of stamina and ideas to entertain her young kids.

"I wish there was such thing as a fast-forward button I could press," she vented once. "I just want to go to sleep, wake up and find this stupid pandemic is over."

"Don't," I replied. "Remember that in a blink, ten years will go by. These days of quarantine will be just a vague memory. And soon *twenty* years will pass, and this will just be a 'fascinating story' we tell new generations—but by then your kids will be grown, and you'll miss these days."

I presented Nathalie with a challenge. I instructed her to fast-forward time in her mind and imagine herself in her nineties, in a nursing home. Her husband would be long dead. Her children would've become grandparents and started to age too. She would be wrinkled and shrunk and arthritic sitting in a rocking chair, complaining that no one came to visit their elderly great-grandma anymore.

Then I asked her to imagine remembering herself at this age.

"I bet you anything you would think. 'Oh, my goodness. What a youthful, hot babe I was back then! I used to have so much energy. And what a wonderful life I had, with a young, virile husband, with two adorable little kids. I would give anything to travel back in time and live one hour there.'

"Well," I concluded, "this is your chance. Your ninety-year-old self has been granted the wish of visiting this time and being young again *just for one hour.* Think about all the things you'd like to do with your husband, your little children, your youthful body. Enjoy this hour deeply—and then take it one hour at a time."

Later on, my sister reported that exercise had helped her dramatically. She shared it with our older sister too, and since then, we created a code phrase we tell each other to remind us to enjoy the present: "Remember the rocking chair."

TIME MACHINE TOOL MEETS CATASTROPHIC THINKING

There's a variant of the Time Machine approach I use to battle catastrophic thinking when I'm allowing my mind to fly to imaginary grim futures.

"What if a hurricane destroys Florida? What if a nuclear war happens? What if another pandemic, this time even worse, occurs?" When using this tool, I allow myself to imagine that whatever tragedy I fear *already happened,* and I've received the joyful gift of traveling in a time machine to enjoy a few more days in this wonderful past.

A SPECIAL TIME TRAVEL TO THE PAST

To illustrate a different way we can use the Time Travel approach, I'd like to tell you the personal story that inspired me to start using this tool.

A couple of years ago, one of my kids unburied a computer file of old photos I hadn't seen in ages. They showed me a decade back in a snowy playground in Chicago. Next to me, my older two boys, then ages four and one, giggled and threw snowballs. But my expression shared none of the joy they radiated.

I studied the younger woman in those pictures with deep compassion—her slumped shoulders, her forced small smile that didn't reach her eyes, the weight of hopelessness in her gaze. Saying that I suffered from seasonal affective disorder would've been an understatement; I loved Chicago, but its winters were literally killing me. And I couldn't escape it because of student visa issues that hung over me, making my professional future uncertain. But my worries didn't end there. I approached the beginning of the end of my former marriage and walked around truly feeling trapped in the wrong lifetime. I remember that time as one of the darkest of my life.

Ten years later, my life had changed dramatically. I'd divorced my ex and happily married my soulmate. I'd moved to the eternal summer of Florida, steps away from the beach; I was now an American citizen, my visa status resolved once and for all. I longed to send a message to the sad young woman in that picture. I wished I could tell her, "Hang in there, sweetie. Everything will get better."

I vanished the photo of my broken self with a click of the mouse, and then the next one brought tears to my eyes. It showed my father playing with his grandchildren in the snow, a mischievous smirk on his face.

I clicked through more images of my dad doing the things he did best: making kids laugh. He pushed swings, and teased, and tickled, and gave piggyback rides while his two grandkids beamed and glowed in absolute bliss. It didn't matter if my children were too little to remember him. Every time their grandpa visited from the Dominican Republic, my kids would instantly latch onto him, as if their DNAs recognized each other. Or perhaps the recognition came from the soul, from a time long before these physical bodies.

In those darker times of my unhappy former marriage, my father's visits from the DR restored health to my soul. He rescued me from my emotional amnesia and reminded me of what real love was. He was a mirror reflecting back to me all the goodness I had long forgotten and a carrier of an unrelenting joy that had become alien for me.

My fingers caressed the screen with bittersweetness and longing. My father had died unexpectedly five years back.

Studying those pictures, I realized that no matter how miserable I'd felt back then, I possessed a treasure I now lacked—a treasure money could not buy, and no other abundant love could replace. I wished I could go back to the past and deliver a different message to that old me. "Hang in there, sweetie. Things will get better in the future. *But whatever you do, don't wish these hard times away.* Enjoy them while they last."

IN SUMMARY

Every moment of our lives, no matter how difficult, contains something good intertwined with the bad. Furthermore, it likely contains something good that we *will not have forever*, something we will miss in the future when we look back at these days. Happiness lies in recognizing those things and savoring them.

EXERCISE

Recreate the exercise I gave my sister. Imagine yourself years from now—perhaps at the end of your life—and then look back at this moment. What part of your present life do you suspect you would miss the most? Go enjoy that! What are the people and animals present in your life today you know you won't have anymore? Go savor them. Can you imagine having less health than you have now? Relish your current health.

Alternatively, if traveling to the future doesn't appeal to you, travel to the past. Just like I did the day I found my father's pictures, can you think of a time in your past when you were truly miserable and dreaming of something you have now? Inhabit that memory for a few minutes, and then imagine your old self praising you and encouraging you to enjoy your great achievements.

15

OTHER TOOLS, BORROWED FROM THE PERSONAL DEVELOPMENT COMMUNITY

T HERE'S NOT ENOUGH SPACE IN this book to present all the great tools I've accumulated over the years—I've devoted decades to my passion for self-improvement. This is a collection of my top favorites.

I'll start with the most important tool of all, so please pay attention.

THE MOST EFFECTIVE SELF-LIFTING TOOL IN THE WORLD: A GRATITUDE JOURNAL

I swear I'm not making it up: I once believed I had invented this tool myself.

It was one of those times in life when I wanted to believe it's darkest just before dawn. My father had died suddenly a few months back. Although my divorce had concluded recently, I still endured dreadful meetings with my ex, as we faced hard financial decisions regarding two properties underwater. On top of that piled the worries about my daughter's seizures, which were acting out as they seemed to always do when I found myself under stress.

One evening, in an emergency attempt to lift my spirits, I re-created an exercise I'd once read in Tony De Mello's book *A Minute of Wisdom*. I grabbed my journal and jotted down all my favorite smells, sights, sounds, textures, and tastes. It took me a couple of days to finish, but it worked so well I kept going. Every night before bed, for a few minutes, I would remind myself of things that made me happy, and that quickly evolved to giving thanks for events that had happened during the day.

"Thank you for the delicious sushi roll I had for lunch."

D Pichardo-Johansson, MD

"Thank you for the rare, peaceful moment reading at my favorite Thai restaurant."

"Thank you for the soft texture of my daughter's hair as I kissed her head goodnight."

"Thank you for the flavor of the teddy graham crackers I nibbled on while making the kids' lunch boxes for tomorrow."

The results amazed me. My mood improved dramatically, and the boost persisted way beyond the few minutes a day the exercise lasted. Knowing I'd be writing my list that night, my brain automatically took note of the good events of my day rather than what was wrong—and it seemed as if what was right multiplied. Coincidence or not, within a couple of months, all the pieces of my life were falling into place. My mediation meetings with the ex were finalized, my daughter was staying out of the hospital, my finances had stabilized, and I was on the right path to recovering from my father's death.

Soon after, I met my future husband, David.

The hippie part of my brain loves to attribute the events to a "Law of Attraction phenomenon." When I changed my thoughts, I became a magnet attracting better things into my life. My scientific brain resists the simplistic explanation but accepts a probable connection: The additional peace that daily exercise gave me allowed me to have a more pleasant attitude during the mediation meetings with my ex, which might've sped up getting into an agreement. It allowed me to relax enough to stop stressing out my daughter, perhaps eliminating the extra adrenaline that could've been contributing to her seizures.

Even more, I don't doubt that dwelling on gratitude also contributed to me grabbing David's attention: A relaxed, trusting person puts out a vibe that's much more attractive than a guarded person. And reminding myself of the things going right in my life gave me the extra edge of confidence to take a leap of faith and accept dating him. Whatever the mechanism, it worked.

I loved that tool so much I started recommending it to my patients, and later on to the doctors in the support group I run; they also reported amazing results. It wasn't until about four years later when one of those doctors in my support group said, "Oh yes, thanks for reminding me of that tool. That's called a gratitude journal. I used to assign them to my depressed patients."

I was blown away to learn that I hadn't invented gratitude journals. Then, ever since, I heard people everywhere talking about them—from Bob Proctor to John Arassaf, to Natalie Ledwell to Oprah, who said she's been keeping them for decades. I can hardly believe I had never heard of them before.

DEMYSTIFYING GRATITUDE JOURNALS

Perfectionism is a handicap. There's no right or wrong way to do gratitude; just get started. The only thermometer to know if you're doing it right is how each entry makes you feel. All of the following items are merely suggestions.

Ideally, get a real journal. Simply reciting things you're thankful for every day will have a positive effect in your life. But I do recommend the habit of *writing them* because it slows you down and makes you savor them a little longer. You can probably jot something on any piece of paper or your regular journal, but I've liked having a journal devoted to that for the additional bonus of being able to re-read previous entries later on; for example, if I'm feeling particularly down and can't come up with what to write. Make a small pleasure out of this: choose a journal that is aesthetically pleasing to you and makes you smile when you see it. My collection of journals has included floral ones, sparkling ones, journals with Bible verses, and journals covered with cat drawings.

Remember. Write the entries in positive terms. "I'm grateful for having food" rather than "I'm grateful I'm not hungry." I only make an exception to that rule if I'm really down or out of material. For example, something I've written more than once is "I'm grateful because I don't have a migraine right now." (I'm serious. Any bad situation I might be facing could be made worse by one of those).

Don't sweat it. I used to feel obligated to write every great thing that had happened to me, which put stress on me. Now, instead, I just commit to writing five things I'm grateful for. More often than not, I end up adding a few bonus entries.

Keep it fresh: Challenge yourself to write original entries rather than repeating what you wrote in previous days. Striving for new material forces us to pay attention to small things we normally take for granted.

And the most important tip: Savor it. Remember that every time you write an entry is an opportunity for neuroplasticity—press the record button for fifteen seconds and re-wire your brain for joy.

I loved a tip a student shared in Natalie Ledwell's online masterclass. She warned not to rush the gratitude journal exercises just to get done with them. I've been guilty of this. She recommended taking the time to write a full sentence, then re-reading each afterward and adding, "Thank you. Thank you. Thank you!" This helps get every drop out of each entry.

In addition to writing full sentences ("I am grateful for my delicious coffee this morning. I am grateful for my son's hug . . ."), you can expand the experience by writing *why* you're grateful for that particular thing. "I am grateful for my A/C *because . . .* it keeps me cool and comfortable in the summer heat."

EXAMPLES

Here are some examples of my gratitude journal entries to get you started. Some entries will be profound and some silly. Some will be long and poetic. Some will be just naming something.

I'm grateful for the glorious quiet moment in the morning when everybody in my house sleeps still, my mind feels refreshed from rest, and I sit with my laptop and my cup of coffee to write.

I'm grateful for the delicious broccoli cheddar soup I had for lunch.

I'm grateful because the hurricane moved away and spared us.

I'm grateful for the time sitting at the breakfast counter having a stimulating chat with my husband.

I'm grateful for the sweet cherries I had earlier.

I'm grateful for the time with my daughter, singing oldies songs out loud in the car.

I'm grateful for how beautiful the full moon looked last night.

I'm grateful for my A/C (because I still remember how hot and muggy it was when we lost power after the last hurricane).

TAPPING

The method of "Meridian tapping" or "EFT" (Emotional Freedom Technique) is another tool directed to help us process feelings and get unstuck in moments of emotional turmoil. It's used both by the psychotherapy and personal development fields. There is a plethora of information online about it, so instead of talking about it in detail here, I'll just provide you with the basic information and some links to get started.

In short, EFT consists of tapping lightly with our fingertips on areas around the face, collar bone, and upper chest that are thought to be acupressure points. As we tap, we repeat our obsessive thoughts, escalating them to the worst-case scenario. After venting those worrisome thoughts for a round or two, we gradually shift to more positive language and end up with, basically, a self pep talk while continuing tapping. The result is a gradual deflating of the intensity of the feelings after each round.

EFT has been used for everything, from releasing limiting beliefs to improving physical symptoms to frank PTSD. I've found it very effective to quiet self-flagellation, reduce fretting, and even used it to help the fatigue after chemotherapy. It might not have helped the actual physical fatigue, but it did relieve my feeling of overwhelm about it, making it much more manageable.

I've been amazed at how well tapping works for me. On the other hand, my teenage son, James, hated it, claiming that it made him feel worse. That first round when we vent our negative thoughts can become quite intense—and that's the purpose. It's a shortcut approach to unburying repressed feelings, and some people don't like to be confronted with them. It's okay. Not every tool will fit everybody.

EFT is popular in New Age circles. People have written book series, hosted seminars, and created careers around teaching EFT to others. I smirk a little bit at this. You don't need a "summit" to learn tapping—anybody can learn to do it within minutes. You can't do it wrong. This is a good video to get started.

Here, *New York Times* bestselling author Jessica Ortner explains the points and the technique. https://www.youtube.com/watch?v=pAclBdj20ZU

AFFIRMATIONS/MANTRAS

To avoid hijacking our own moods, we must carefully monitor our language and inner dialogue. If you study yourself, you'll notice that every setback in your life seems to reactivate the same old internal dialogue, rooted in old wounds. That dialogue comes as different flavors of, "I'm not enough."

"I'm an impostor."

"I'm never going to get ahead."

"Nobody cares for me."

"Nobody appreciates me."

Acute events would automatically trigger memories of our early wounds by activating the oldest parts of our brain associated with survival—the limbic system, and specifically the amygdala, the brain region that records trauma. The wound doesn't have to be serious trauma to become engraved in the subconscious memory with the same intensity of life-threatening events.

A silly example from my personal life: During childhood, my older sister used to accuse me of being annoying and uncool. That message got reinforced later on in high school when I felt unwelcome by the popular kids. Those events created a negative inner dialogue saying, "I'm unpopular. The cool kids don't like to play with me." Drastically different life issues can trigger these monologues—from a clash with a friend to a slow business season to a disappointing result in a book launch.

A more insidious example? I grew up in a Third World country where corrupt government authorities routinely rigged elections and stole government funds (and for a while, murdered anyone who protested about it). Public services never worked. We rarely had electricity or running water, but complaining about it achieved nothing. What was worse, I grew up surrounded by deep poverty. Every day I saw kids my age on the streets—barefoot, half-naked, and hungry. I ached from the inability to help them. These moments of my life created a deep wound of powerlessness that never seemed to heal fully.

For most of my adult life, whenever I faced serious obstacles to a goal, I spiraled down to an internal dialogue of powerlessness. "Why do I even try? Nothing ever changes. The game is rigged against me, and nothing I do will make a difference."

How do I stop that inner dialogue when it starts dragging me down? Tapping/EFT works great to break the loop but might be impractical in the middle of a business meeting. Affirmations are a good rescue option and also help with brain retraining or neuroplasticity.

AFFIRMATIONS: FINDING THE DEEPER TRUTH

The practice of affirmations consists of crafting sentences in positive, uplifting language to neutralize that negative internal dialogue we default to. For a while, the word "affirmations" made me roll my eyes. They sounded like self-lies, were just too time-consuming, and I couldn't stick to them. The particular method I'd learned called for repeating your affirmations thirty times a day for thirty days and then eleven extra times for every time you slipped and said something negative ("to neutralize it"). It helped a little but proved exhausting.

Instead, I've found it more practical to create positive sentences I can repeat again and again as a mantra when I run into negative thinking. Hopefully, you can find your own happy medium between those two extremes of discipline and laziness.

But my biggest breakthrough came when I heard bestselling author and transformational speaker Lisa Nichols recommend a twist. Instead of saying the opposite of what you normally say, she encourages you to search for *the deeper truth*.

For example, when I catch my inner voice repeating, "I'm powerless," trying to bulldoze my way over it with "I'm powerful" doesn't help me. Instead, I search deeper and find something that does feel true. "My small efforts compound, and my consistency pays off." Later on, I've evolved to a more empowering mantra, "I've conquered so much in the past; I can tackle anything."

Many authors have different variations of affirmations and mantras. I really like Tony Robbins' version, "Incantations," where he combines the words with an enthusiastic tone and invigorating body movements—but of course, those require more energy.

And speaking of different variations and options, let's talk about one last tool you have to improve your joy capacity—the biggest yet.

SELF-EDUCATION - BOOKS, COURSES, AND MENTORS

I spent over a decade of my life in medical training, between med school, internal medicine residency, and a Hem-Onc fellowship. And that's only the beginning! I must've spent thousands of hours studying, learning skills, and taking tests. Well, I once decided that if I'd spent such a large portion of my life studying to earn a living, it made even more sense that I studied how to be a happier person—so whatever living I earned was worth it. I never regretted that decision and encourage you to make it too.

Think about it—if schools teach us things like World War II history and trigonometry, doesn't it make even more sense that we study how to heal our past wounds, take control of our moods, and achieve goals? I went through a phase when I used to read one self-help book a week. A self-help book can never replace professional therapy, but in my case, it did complement it. Every good book I read helped me see my unhealthy patterns more clearly and gave me the tools to create a better life. At best, they planted new seeds, and at worst, they fertilized others previously planted, cementing messages in my mind. From self-help, I shifted to personal development, but the learning process continues. When reading isn't an option, I resort to online masterclasses, webinars, or podcasts I can listen to while commuting or doing chores.

If you're reading this book, I dare to guess you're someone who likes nourishing the mind. Well, great news! Never before in history has it been easier to get access to so much free information than now—you only need to Google a topic or type a few words on YouTube. However, with all these resources at our fingertips, deciding whom to believe can be overwhelming.

With so many experts out there, how do we know who to trust? Simply choose what resonates with you at a deep level. Our favorite writers, speakers, and "gurus" have to click with us at a gut level. If the one you're listening to doesn't ignite you, just move on. Don't worry. There are plenty of options to choose from.

A quote attributed to Lao Tzu states, "When the student is ready, the teacher will appear." I believe that phenomenon also applies to books.

More than once, at a bookstore or library, I've felt a gravitational pull to a shelf where I found a book that proved exactly what I needed to read. I once feared that the disappearance of the physical bookstore would end those occurrences, but it hasn't been the case. One of the most life-changing audiobooks I've listened to in my life, *Conversations with God* by Neal Donald Walsh, came to me years after its publication in the most unexpected place, a *discount clothing store*. Don't ask me why that one box of old-fashioned CDs was there for sale. Also, the Universe has many ways to get our attention, usually through coincidences and through repetition of the same message from different sources (pay extra attention when that happens).

Just like when you're looking for a new romantic partner, the best action is to keep doing things you enjoy and be receptive to the messages around you. Keep showing up to the right places, and you'll create a force that will keep your hunger for knowledge well fed. One day a Facebook ad pops in that invites you to sign up for a free masterclass, and you do. That leads to hearing about a book or a speaker you never heard before and ordering their book. The speaker now has you on their email list and keeps sending you inspirational messages and introducing other influencers. Just like hanging around with the wrong people damages us, the more we listen to uplifting people and read good material, the more our baseline mood will rise.

IF YOU NEED HELP GETTING STARTED:

One of the best decisions you can make to jumpstart growth in your life is working with someone one in one. A mentor or a Life Coach like me can help you apply mood management tools in a way that's individualized for your circumstances. If you would like to have a clarity session with me, which is a complimentary call to figure out if we would be a good fit, you can schedule it at www.joyfullysuccessful.com

Besides that, here's a partial list of authors that have helped me in difficult moments. It was difficult to choose, so I just listed the *finest pearls*. If you Google their names, the browser will also offer you other names people have searched for.

For healing childhood and trauma: John Bradshaw, Ph.D. (I strongly recommend his book *Homecoming: Healing the Inner Child*, and also his book *Healing the Shame that Binds You*.)

For improving romantic relationships: Harville Hendrix. Gay and Kathlyn Hendricks, John Gray (yes, the famous *Venus and Mars* guy).

For reconnecting with spirituality in a way that does not put down religion: Marianne Williamson (*A Return to Love* and *A Women's Worth* are my favorite books of hers). Neale Donald Walsh (*Conversations with God*). Iyanla Vanzant.

To learn more about neuroplasticity and rewiring the brain: Dr. Rick Hanson (*Hardwiring Happiness*).

For hitting the reset button, cheering you up when you think you're uncheerable: Eckhart Tolle, Esther/Abraham Hicks (a little controversial, as it involves "channeling messages," but worth listening to with an open mind).

For recovering faith in humanity: Brene Brown (and all her research on vulnerability).

For helping with addictions (even the legal ones such as our cell phones): Russell Brandt.

For goal-achieving: Tony Robbins, Natalie Ledwell and her Ultimate Success Masterclass.

For inspiration/motivation: Lisa Nichols, most interviews Oprah ever gave, Will Smith's YouTube video on dream achieving, Denzel Washington's Life Advice speech.

WHAT'S NEXT

Hopefully, this chapter has helped you widen your tool collection and get you started in your search for more. But even the sharpest tools are useless if we leave them forgotten in the shed and never touch them.

Why is it that so often we know intellectually what we're supposed to do—yet don't do it?

In the next chapters, we'll address the most common blocks that keep us from utilizing the tools we've learned.

16
TROUBLESHOOTING 101: "NOTHING WORKS."

PERHAPS YOU'VE COME THIS FAR in the book and still feel nothing I've said applies to you. Maybe you feel no better than when you began, and you're giving me one last chance before ditching the book.

Take a deep breath. It's okay.

Some concepts might take time to germinate in the soil of the mind.

If you don't feel the joy taking root yet, hang in there; it takes as much repetition as mastering an instrument. Later on, when you least expect it, you'll hear something that echoes the lessons in this book and will finally be ready to grasp these concepts. Especially, be patient if you're reading this during a low time, when we wear the opposite of rose-colored-glasses and everything we encounter sucks.

On the other hand, you might be simply experiencing a mental block. We all have them. And releasing them is as satisfying as identifying a small pebble that had gotten trapped in the gadgets and cogwheels of factory machinery. It might be something small, but it's enough to mess up the entire mechanism, and dislodging it can make a huge difference.

A small tweak might be all you're missing to fully open the gates to receive joy back into your life. In this section, we'll touch on some frequent blocks and how to navigate them. And I'm going to start with what I considered the biggest block of all. It's so important that I decided to devote a whole chapter to it. Are you ready?

THE BIGGEST QUESTION YOU HAVE TO ASK YOURSELF: DO YOU REALLY (REALLY, REALLY) WANT TO BE HAPPY?

Resistance can manifest in many different ways. Let's take a book like this as an example. You go through the trouble of buying a book, then never read it, or quit it halfway without explanation. Your to-do list keeps getting in the way of retaking it—you're not making up an excuse. You truly are busy. Though we legitimately quit books when we can't relate to them, often we do the same thing when the opposite happens, and they hit too close to home. Maybe you do finish the book but don't do any of the exercises. Or you do them halfway or half-heartedly, or for a short time, and then assume they don't work.

And finishing a book is something with relatively low stakes! Worst-case scenario, we read a so-so book, we wasted some time. Imagine how much more we'll resist taking risky action that can shake our lives.

Please ask yourself this question and then answer with brutal honesty: "Do I really want to be happier?"

Anything less than a wholehearted, immediate "Yes!" hints at resistance. Even if your answer is "Yes, *but* . . ." It doesn't matter how righteously justified the "but" is. Pay attention to your answers.

"But instead, I should be happy with what I already have."

"But I know life is hard and happiness is elusive."

"But I once had my chance to be happy and blew it."

We can't make a new habit stick if we're giving ourselves conflicting information or have an unconscious agenda. We'll sabotage ourselves over and over.

Unconscious agendas can take many shapes, and here I share some of them.

ARE YOU TRYING TO PUNISH YOURSELF FOR SOMETHING, OR DON'T YOU BELIEVE YOU DESERVE HAPPINESS?

Take a long hard inventory at yourself. Write down anything you've done you haven't forgiven yourself for. Also, pay attention to any negative inner dialogue or derogatory messages you heard growing up. Then take a wild stretch and ask yourself: Is it possible that I'm unable to change my situation because I don't believe I deserve happiness? If that is the case, you're not alone. You'd be surprised how common this is.

I once realized that I was blocking myself from finding love after my divorce because I hadn't forgiven myself for ending my marriage vows. I'd once sworn to be by my ex's side for the rest of my life, and now I had deserted him. I had to grieve that, allow myself to feel the feelings of sadness, shame, and regret. And then, following the advice of Debbie Ford in her book *Spiritual Divorce*, I wrote "Divorce vows" for my ex. "I, Diely, take you, X, as my ex-husband. I promise always to respect you and never bad-mouth you. I promise to be a good co-parent for our children and foster their love for you . . ." The relief that followed that step was amazing. Shortly after, I was finally able to tackle that task I had avoided for months: signing up for online dating. Within three months, I met my husband.

DOES A PART OF YOU BELIEVE YOU'RE BETRAYING SOMEONE BY BEING TOO HAPPY?

This is similar to the previous section. To explain the difference, I'll give you another personal example. In the past, I held myself back from true financial success because of guilt about my origins. I grew up in the Dominican Republic, seeing barefoot, half-naked children my age beg for money on the streets. Even my parents' childhoods were stories of poverty, hunger, and child labor. I felt guilty all my life for the unearned privilege of having been born to a family who had the means to feed me, keep me dressed, and give me an education.

For someone else, the answer would've been logical "Come on! Do you really think that by staying poor, you would ever help anyone? On the contrary, the more money you make, the more people you can help." Still, it took me years to work through that guilt. The good news is that just bringing something from unconsciousness to awareness starts making a difference.

ARE YOU AFRAID OF SUCCESS OR HAPPINESS AND SABOTAGING YOUR EFFORTS IS A WAY TO REMAIN AT THIS LEVEL?

Sometimes we say we want something, but we're afraid of how our lives will change once we obtain it. For years my friend Marie claimed she wanted to become a successful romance author, yet the moment her books began taking off, she encountered writer's block and stopped writing or promoting for two years. Later on, as she resumed writing, she admitted that she might've been scared by how quickly things were going. "I was afraid at that rate, I would never have time for my family."

If you suspect this might be your case, I recommend applying the Truth Serum. Here, you engage in a journaling session where you're only allowed to write the truth and nothing but the truth. The key here continues to be brutal honesty to yourself.

ARE YOU SO AFRAID OF CHANGE YOU'D RATHER BE MISERABLE THAN TAKING A NEW ACTION?

My friend Julissa babysat for me while "looking for a job"—for about five years. Her babysitting gig allowed her just enough money to get by while not having to face the real world of angry bosses, co-workers, and taxes. Needless to say, her efforts to find a job were half-hearted at best.

Sometimes we don't have enough incentive to change our lives until the pain of a situation is greater than the pain of taking action—until we touch bottom. High-achievers like you (and I know you are one because you're reading this book) don't allow themselves to touch bottom and therefore don't often get the impulse to take drastic action.

It would take another whole book to address the fear of change—trust me; it has paralyzed me more than once. I've learned that, short of touching bottom, the best we can do is work on self-love, so we raise our own bar of what we would tolerate.

Luckily, with age comes wisdom. More often than not, if we stumble down the same roads enough times, we eventually learn that the pain of staying in soul-sucking situations is not worth it. But you don't want to wait to be near the end of your life to be happy right? To be happy *now*, start exercising the muscle of change.

EXERCISING THE MUSCLE OF CHANGE

I've studied mental flexibility when educating myself on autism in order to help my daughter. Like most kids on the spectrum, she loves repetitive games where the exact same plot happens again and again. As part of her therapy, I play with her and don't try to dismantle her rigid routines, but I introduce one small change at a time—for example, by making a stuffed animal do something crazy and funny. She now loves it and looks forward to the surprises. The recipe for success has been: 1-) The change has to be small and gradual. 2-) At first, it has to be fun.

Start in an innocuous way. Wear your ring or watch on the opposite hand, or wear a different outfit just because. Change your route to work. If you've always owned round plates, buy yourself some square ones. Then practice neuroplasticity, savoring the feeling of success. The key is to prove to yourself you *can* embrace change, encouraging you to push a little further every day.

And remember the saying: courage is not lacking fear; it's acting despite it.

ARE YOU SECRETLY ENJOYING YOUR BAD MOOD/SITUATION AND WOULD RATHER REVEL IN IT THAN CHANGE IT?

Can we be addicted to a negative feeling? I believe we can.

Sometimes, our reluctance to improve a situation is deeper than the fear of change. We secretly enjoy our misery—we have become addicted to the self-pity or the bittersweetness of melancholy. Perhaps we're even hooked on the indirect rewards of having people express us their commiseration or support.

By the way, this is a very short-lived reward. One of the first mental health lectures I received in medical school described the dismal difference in caregivers' attitudes when helping a loved one with an acute illness or a chronic one. Once an illness (or a negative attitude, or self-commiseration) perpetuates, caregivers start losing their stamina, often resenting the sick person. (This doesn't mean they're not "good people," it just means they're human). So, I don't recommend being unhappy as a way to earn support.

Start by telling yourself the truth, the whole truth, and nothing but the truth. Maybe you'll surprise yourself by concluding, "Now that I think about it, I *don't* want anything to change in my life," and the whole gift of this book might be that you decide to look at your so-called negative situation with different, more receptive eyes. I liked the answer Harvard psychologist

Dr. Ron Siegel gave in an online conference I watched. Several therapists brainstormed what to do when clients seemed stuck, and everything else had failed. Dr. Siegel replied, "I tell them, enjoy it. I tell them: You'll stop being stuck when it stops being interesting."

But if you're still reading this book, I'm going to take a wild guess that a part of you does want to change your situation and improve your mood. What I recommend is applying the concept of neuroplasticity, rewiring your brain. Like a physical therapist working with reconditioning the muscles of a stroke survivor, teach yourself to feel joy again little by little. Pay attention to those moments in the day when you do feel joyful and savor them. Press the pause button. Dwell on them. Stretch them. Replay them in your mind. Make yourself a mental note of "See how good this feels?" Tell yourself: "There it is! This is evidence that I can feel joy."

A simple way to get started is to return to the Joy Menu we created in the first part of this book. Introduce a couple of pleasant activities every single day, then hit the record button while doing them to foster neuroplasticity.

YOU'VE EARNED ANOTHER BADGE!

Congratulations on completing the basic course on troubleshooting happiness! Are you ready for the advanced classes? As you continue to earn your advanced degree in joy, we'll be discussing other roadblocks and how to overcome them.

17

TROUBLESHOOTING 201: "I CAN'T MAKE ANY OF THIS STICK."

D ECIDING TO CHANGE SOMETHING REQUIRES courage. Then, sticking to that decision and not backsliding proves even more challenging.

Why is it that it's so difficult to hold on to new resolutions? In this chapter, we'll explore a common issue affecting the human condition, the inability to *sustain* change. From losing weight to finding inner peace, the following concepts will help you forever.

Are you ready? Here we go.

"I CAN'T MAKE ANY OF THIS STICK."

One of the most common complaints I hear is, "All this sounds good in theory, but the truth is that I've tried it before. It works well for a brief time, and then I can't get myself to do it with discipline." I've been there. For years I beat myself up for being unable to stick to an exercise program or a meditation program. Or for picking up the same bad habit over and over after having sworn I would quit it (from excess shopping to overreacting to criticism).

Remember the prerequisite course. Check if your inability to stick to good habits comes from fear, resistance, or a tendency to self-sabotage. Whether the answer is yes or no, keep reading.

DISCIPLINE

Will Smith has a wonderful speech about self-discipline I love to play for my sons (I encourage you to watch it on YouTube). He says that ninety-nine percent of people don't achieve success because they lack the habit of discipline. And he compares discipline not to punishment but self-love. "I love you too much to let you eat that pizza." (https://www.youtube.com/watch?v=ft_DXwgUXB0)

However, I admit that for someone not blessed with a strong sense of discipline, that may come as a tall order. It's like a bodybuilder telling an untrained person, "Bench-pressing four hundred pounds is not a big deal."

The good news is that there are a couple of shortcuts to becoming a disciplined person. I'll share the more scientific first and the most powerful second. Ready?

1. DISCIPLINE STARTS WITH SMALL, PLEASURABLE CHANGES.

I could bore you to death raving about the online lecture on the neurophysiology of addiction I recently completed. A Harvard professor explained how the centers of pleasure and survival in our brain are strongly connected with the pre-frontal brain cortex. This site controls all our higher functions, including discipline and problem-solving. An addict whose brain has been fried by drugs and is hopeless to function would perform amazingly complicated tasks and schemes to get his next drug fix. And it's all boosted by brain chemical changes (dopamine) in the pleasure pathways.

The bottom line: we'll go to great lengths and tolerate tons of pain on behalf of an activity that brings us a sense of pleasure and reward. Please notice that this is different from "bribing," such as rewarding yourself with a treat *after* you performed a dreadful beneficial task; that gets old soon. Here I'm referring to when the beneficial task *is* the source of pleasure.

I was unable to break my blocks against exercising until I found the one exercise that brought me joy and pleasure. Contrary to other forms of exercise I dreaded, bicycling gave me instant gratification—watching the scenery go by and feeling the refreshing wind in my face. The more I got into it, the more I appreciated its calming effects in my brain. I was hooked long before I noticed the positive physical effects, such as improved stamina and focus. Later on, the repeated association of bike riding with well-being allowed me to open my mind to other ways of fitness.

That's the reason why in Part I of the book, I strongly encouraged you to put on your joy lists only activities that made your heart skip a beat. You'll be much more likely to stick to your new joy routines if you wholeheartedly love them.

Before attempting to change a habit or achieve a goal, be brutally honest: Do you hate this activity? Would you rather ditch this goal and change it to one you do have a chance of sticking to? Creating a new habit is easier if we follow the path of least resistance. Like my friend Chuck the contractor used to say, "You can only eat an elephant one bite at a time. Take the sweet bite first."

Exercise 1: The hardest part of every task is getting started. Choose one small change to your everyday routine that feels more pleasurable and effortless (add a new joy task or throw a pleasurable twist into something you're already doing daily). Cement that one before moving to the next one. The saying, "It takes thirty days to create a habit," is only one arbitrary cutoff. You decide if you want to introduce something new every week or every other week. Once you create momentum, it will be easier to stick to the less pleasant changes.

Each time you remember to perform your new task, give yourself credit and savor it to allow for neuroplasticity. You'll be surprised by how quickly changes add on and how it gets easier every time.

Pro Tip: Create new good habits by tying them to an already established habit. For example, one of my most firmly established routines is brushing my teeth before going to bed. I could never forget to do it because I feel restless until I do. When I started taking daily medication for breast cancer treatment, I was afraid I'd constantly forget (I'd been healthy all my life and never took pills). The solution was placing the pill holder next to my toothbrush in the bathroom. Placing things next to my toothbrush has worked like magic for any new bedtime routine I want to add— from skincare to developing the habit of listening to an educational or inspirational lecture or podcast at bedtime.

This trick is especially effective if that old habit you're tying the new one to is one that brings you pleasure. For example, like many people, I have a strong attachment to my cell phone and rarely forget it. So when I kept forgetting my wallet at home, I replaced it with a wallet/phone case containing my cell. I never forgot it again. When the COVID pandemic started, and I was having trouble remembering to carry hand sanitizer with me, I tied a travel-size hand sanitizer bottle to the belt clip where I carry my Air pods.

2. THE MOST EFFECTIVE DISCIPLINE BOOST IN THE WORLD: ALIGNMENT

Contrary to bench-pressing four hundred pounds—which might take years of training—we all have inside us the ability to gather instant strength and discipline when emergency circumstances require it. I bet you've already done it at least once in your life. Have you ever surprised yourself by doing something you once thought impossible? Ran faster and jumped higher than you ever thought possible to rescue your child from being run over by a car on the street? Stayed up all night to pass a test or solve a problem? Procrastinated something until the very last minute and then pulled it off when it seemed improbable?

What is that magic combination we dial in to achieve something that had been previously unachievable? I will need to write a separate book to dissect that (and I may). But here, I will only give you the simplest answer: We tap into our *higher self* by aligning *passion* with our *deepest values* and then shut down resistance.

Think about it: Maybe the passion came from the terror and adrenaline of the moment (you passionately wanted to survive, or rescue your kid, or pass this test). Maybe it came from wanting something with all your heart. The bottom line was that it came from *caring a whole lot*. Nobody with the "I don't care" attitude accomplishes anything big. (Which, by the way, "I don't care" is not the same as being detached from the outcome, which does help). That passion can only be channeled full throttle (resistance eliminated) when it's in alignment with our core values and our strongest convictions. Take the example of the person who rescued her child from being run over: The core value of love came to play, along with the absolute conviction that keeping her child alive is the only acceptable option.

RECONNECTING WITH YOUR PASSIONS AND VALUES

Like in the previous section where we talked about tying your new desired habit to something you enjoy, you can boost your chance for success if you tie any goal to something you really, *really,* care about—your passions and core values. In Chapter 13, I provided a link to get you started with that.

Another tool I truly recommend is the exercise of the "Seven Levels of Why." I encourage you to Google it. I heard the concept for the first time from Dean Graziosi, but according to the Internet, it was developed by Kurt Greening. In this process, you keep asking yourself why you want to do something again and again until you find its root at your core. For example, take my answers to the question, "Why do you want to write a self-help book about joy."

Level 1: Because I truly believe the world needs joy, and I want people to hear about this.

Level 2: And why do you want people to hear about this? Answer: Because I want to touch lives.

Level 3: And why do you want to touch lives? Because I want to make a difference in the world.

Level 4: And why do you want to make a difference in the world? Because I didn't feel I could make a difference while working fifteen years in oncology.

Level 5: And why didn't you make a difference? Because working with some of the saddest cases imaginable left me raw and worn out.

Level 6: And why were you raw and worn out? Because I felt powerless to make a difference, and it was painful.

Level 7: And why was that painful? Because it reminded me of the powerlessness I felt all my childhood to make a difference for the people around me, suffering hunger and poverty in a Third World country.

As you may notice, the first few levels sound honorable enough and appear to be deep, but the deeper you go, the more *personal* it becomes. Invariably, if you answer with the truth, you'll run into one of your core wounds. And once you connect with that, the effect is similar to that emergency situation where you tap into speed and strength you never imagined possible.

Exercise 2: Yes, you guessed it. Pick the most important goal or project you have in your life right now and go ahead and practice the Seven Levels of Why.

Exercise 3: Emulate the first step of any twelve-step program. Do a prayer or meditation, or casual conversation with your Higher Power, saying, "In the past, I've been powerless to change or stick to a disciplined program. But today, I'm surrendering this into your hands." Next, align what you want to accomplish with your highest passions and values. If one of your values is family, align your desire for greater joy in your life to the knowledge that you'll be a much better parent/spouse if you're a joyful person.

IN SUMMARY (AND A WORD ON CONSISTENCY)

Yes, even if in the past you've attempted to make changes in your life and failed, it is possible to break that cycle. Start with small, pleasurable changes you're more likely to stick to. It definitely helps to align new goals with our deepest values and passions and to tie new habits to other well-cemented routines.

Be patient with yourself. Don't beat yourself up if you derailed and stopped your new habit. Ask yourself, "Did I stop because deep inside, I don't want to make this change?" If the answer is yes, pick a different goal. If the answer is no, pick yourself up and start again. And again. And again.

Repetition is key. And every time you reward and acknowledge yourself for small successes, you create new brain connections. Often, those go unnoticed until a tilting point is reached, and then suddenly, everything gets much easier. It's similar to a child who couldn't walk yesterday, then connects one more neuron today and can. It took months and months of practice, but when the change happens, it's like a switch flipped.

And if you're still noticing resistance, keep reading and don't despair. The solution might be in the next chapter, "Troubleshooting 301."

18
TROUBLESHOOTING 301: MISCELLANEOUS BLOCKS

F INALLY! THIS IS THE PART where you're allowed to cherry-pick. Keep skimming until you find a topic that appeals to you or fits your situation. Ready? Here we go.

1. I FEEL THAT NOTHING IN THIS BOOK APPLIES TO ME.

I've shared many times the lessons on perspective I learned when my nine-year-old son crashed my husband's car. Every so often, someone misses the point and says, "Well, that doesn't apply to me because I don't have children." Other times, when I share how I reinvented my life after my divorce, someone says, "Well, I'm against breaking marriages, so I can't relate to that story." If I failed to make this concept clear earlier, please allow me to clarify now: *There are many different ways to be happy.* The examples in this book about finding joy have nothing to do with the specific situations and everything to do with the *process* of psychological transformation needed to achieve the goal. Whatever your personal difficulties, this process *will* benefit you

I invite you to see beyond the form into the *essence* of each story and look at them as metaphors, the same way you might view a story about slaying dragons or learning to fly on eagles' wings.

Let's take life companionship. Perhaps you're someone who has chosen to remain single, or someone who seeks a same-sex partner and is tired of hearing stories about women searching for Prince Charming. You may feel tempted to roll your eyes when I get starry-eyed talking about the miracle of meeting my husband, David. Instead, see it as a story of deciding to find happiness against all odds. I was a single mother of *four,* including twins with special needs, living in a town of elderly retirees and carrying emotional baggage. I'd married my first and last boyfriend, so I had no idea how to tackle the dating world. Nobody thought I would ever find a man willing to accept my baggage. Do you see the real message behind the story? "Never listen to the pessimists."

Or let's take the story of leaving my oppressive ex-husband. It's not really about getting a divorce (when the statistics say the odds of something are fifty-fifty, it's hard to argue it's anything extraordinary). It's about breaking the chains that held me back from listening to my heart. This implied:

1. I learned to speak the truth to myself about what I was really feeling at each given time.

2. I took a hard look at all the concepts I had been spoon-fed throughout my life to differentiate which were real values and which were simply taboos and beliefs from the people who raised me.

3. Instead of following "the rules," I learned to follow *my inner compass.* In other words, if it makes me feel *miserable,* I walk away from it; if it makes my soul soar, I walk toward it. (How did something that simple take me decades to understand?)

So, focus on the feelings of being stuck I describe in each example and ask yourself, "Have I ever felt like this, even if in a completely different scenario?" Then study the changes in thought pattern each breakthrough took and ask yourself my favorite question. "Which lesson do *I* need to learn from this situation to graduate from it and move on?"

2. I FEEL NUMB

Numbness is a frequent result of trauma or hurt, and it makes all the sense in the world. Of course, our psyches will protect themselves from pain by blocking all feeling.

Obligatory disclaimer: Numbness may arise from the mechanism of defense of dissociation, where we will detach from the situation or trauma as if it had happened to someone else and not us. Sometimes it may be covering for severe trauma (for example, sexual abuse), and trying to tackle it alone might be unsafe. If you suspect that is your case, I strongly encourage you to get professional help.

Usually, numbness feels like a blessed relief and the smart choice for our minds. As we mentioned in the section about denial, it often allows us to endure situations that would have broken us in the past. I compare it to the numbness we sometimes feel during extreme exercise: if we were running for our lives through the jungle, it makes sense to block the pain in our joints and muscles until we are safe.

However, while numbness has its place in traumatic situations, it can also become an obstacle to healing. As I've mentioned before: we must feel the pain to process the emotions. If we don't allow ourselves to do this, the unprocessed emotions can become an abscess in our souls. We can treat ourselves with pain medication and can take antibiotics for the rest of our lives, but the problem will resurface again and again. Only when we drain the abscess can the antibiotics reach the infected site through the blood supply and heal it.

So, if you're not in the middle of a life-and-death emergency that requires you to feel numb to survive—and as long as you're not dealing with the severe type of trauma we mentioned earlier—I strongly encourage you to relieve that numbness and confront what it conceals.

Have a conversation with yourself. I recommend doing it in writing by hand, because research points to it helping us connect the right and left-brain hemispheres, enhancing the processing. Whether in writing or verbally, ask yourself: What are the feelings and emotions you think you might be blocking with this numbness? Is it sadness? Anger? Fear? Regret? Dig into it without running away from it by starting your entry with the title, "The truth, the whole truth, and nothing but the truth." Speak the unspeakable. Tell yourself the ugly things you've been avoiding.

"Wait a minute! That's masochism!" you may protest. My husband, David, will be the first to claim that digging in the past by reminding ourselves about our traumas is unhealthy. Yet even he would praise the value of *catharsis*.

A SOLUTION TO NUMBNESS: CATHARSIS

Remember the word catharsis? I like to say that catharsis is poking a sleeping monster in *indirect* ways, usually through art. If you do not like the idea of journaling or digging into your feelings, then take catharsis as a different approach.

Start with the same question. What are the feelings and emotions that you think you might be blocking with this numbness? Is it sadness? Then make yourself cry by watching a tear-jerker movie or reading a moving novel. Is the feeling you're blocking perhaps anger? Get a pair of boxing gloves and hit a punching bag. Is it fear? Watch a movie that describes the worst-case scenario you're terrified of (in my case, it would be stories about mothers dying of cancer).

It might feel scary at first but take my word for it: You'll be okay. It's not true that once you allow yourself to release the hold just for one minute, you'll be unable to regain control ever again.

If you've been holding things in for a long time, it might take you a while to let go, but trust me, once you emerge on the other side, you will feel deeply relieved and much closer to your recovery and healing. Many of my patients and clients who did this exercise described it as being "washed clean" by the rain.

3. "DIGGING INTO FEELINGS IS JUST NOT MY THING."

My beloved husband and I have learned to agree to disagree on the subject of healing past hurt. He jokes, "I'm not into digging out feelings. I'd rather crush them in my feelings-grinder brain device."

I strongly believe that unburying hidden feelings and learning to follow our inner guidance is the best way to find happiness. Do you have to believe it? Hell no. At the risk of repeating myself, I'll reiterate: there's no wrong way to be happy. And if you've been doing something that works for you and you feel fully satisfied with the results, you don't have to listen to anybody else's method.

But I'm going to take a wild guess that if you're reading this book, it means you're not one hundred percent satisfied with your life. Or at least, you're looking to increase your arsenal of resources for bouncing back from adversity. With that in mind, I dare to suggest one last time that you give the catharsis strategies I mentioned in the last section a try. If you're still unconvinced, I invite you to continue reading with an open mind, taking and leaving from the tools presented. I guarantee you that you will get something out of this book—even if only one new tool or new angle to look at an old idea.

4. I'M TOO DAMAGED TO BE HAPPY

Back to that obligatory disclaimer. Perhaps you're reading these tools and saying, "These pieces of advice are ridiculous considering everything I've gone through." If you're a veteran with PTSD, a survivor of childhood violence, sexual abuse, or any other severe traumatic event, you'll also need professional mental help.

Most adults have some degree of mild PTSD (for example: we refuse to date people who look or sound like our exes). But if you suffer severe PTSD (a memory which causes racing heart, dissociation, fright . . .), then I strongly recommend you combine what you're learning in this book with formal therapy or with physician-supervised medication if needed. Otherwise, using these tools would be like taking Tylenol to treat a fever instead of treating the infection causing the fever. You want to feel better, so it's okay to take the Tylenol. But you also have to work on the infection.

I'm a believer in therapy. If you've tried talk therapy and been unimpressed or consider it too slow for your taste, I encourage you to try a different flavor. There are many different options that don't focus on the past as much as on giving you life skills (such as the different types of behavioral therapy). There's even hypnotherapy, which many people I know have described as a great shortcut to uncover unconscious memories and heal them (I've had a few hypnotherapy sessions myself and was impressed).

You may ask, "What if therapy is absolutely not an option for me? What if I can't afford it, or if the idea of disclosing intimate stuff to a stranger turns me inside out? Can I try to heal myself reading self-help books?" Legally, here I have to say, "No. Nobody with a truly traumatic history should attempt digging in the past alone." The truth? If you're truly committed to healing, nothing is impossible. But trying to heal psychologically by yourself—without help—would miss the most important part of therapy, which is human connection. I heard a therapist once say that ninety-nine percent of the effect of therapy comes from the experience of unconditional love and acceptance. Bottom line? You know yourself better than anyone else, and you're welcome to check the self-help books I recommended in

Chapter 15. But the most important thing that you'll need for healing is reaching out to someone who cares and can give you perspective about the past you're trying to heal. If you don't have someone like that in your life, join a support group of people who have gone through something similar to what you did. Those are sometimes the source of tremendous healing and lifelong friendships.

5. I'M EXPECTING TERRIBLE THINGS IN MY FUTURE

Someone reading this book may feel entitled to say, "None of this helps me. I've been diagnosed with a terrible illness that is likely to cost me my life or leave me handicapped. How can I face every day when I know things are only going downhill from now?"

Take a deep breath. I cover that more in the section about facing a chronic or life-threatening illness. But in the meantime, the answer I'm going to give you is so simple I suspect you might roll your eyes and accuse me of falling into a cliché: You have to learn to live in the present moment.

You might be saying, "Come on! That's such hippie-dippy stuff!" Advising someone to stay in the moment is like an acrobat telling a regular person, "Go ahead, it's easy. Do a triple jump on the trapeze." Easy to say, but no one can do it.

Please bear with me. I encourage you to read Chapters 13 and 14, where I explain how I used the Time Machine approach to stay in the present after my diagnosis and other challenges. In the last section of this book, I elaborate on different scenarios, including living with a chronic illness or a death sentence.

6. "I FEEL SILLY/EMBARRASSED/UNCOOL DOING THESE EXERCISES."

Sometimes, I make the mistake of trying to cheer up a friend who doesn't want to be cheered up. A knee-jerk response I get is, "This unicorns-and-rainbows stuff is not for me." Or "I can't be Pollyanna." This is often a simple example of someone who likes feeling miserable (there's nothing I can do about that). But other times, the person truly feels self-conscious. They've bought into the world's belief that showing effusive joy or enthusiasm is uncool.

In my opinion, being cool is overrated, especially if it gets in the way of being happy.

When I was growing up, many people (my older sister included) considered me way too sweet for their taste. The fashion of the time was the tough woman. From the rebel punk of the eighties when I was just a child, to the *whatever* culture of the nineties, to the sexually liberated woman of *Sex and the City* in the 2000s—it seemed like the heroines of pop culture were my antithesis. Though I'm proud to say I'm a pretty strong and resilient human being, to me, strength had never equaled being "in your face."

The bottom line is: we're all different. And it makes sense that we seek and enjoy different experiences because we're all different organs (or cells) in the body of God. If *every* suggestion in this book turns your insides out, it simply means this book is not for you. Don't waste one more second of your precious time reading it.

But if this is not a lost cause, and the problem is that *some* of the items on my list of joyful activities left you cold (or irked you), by all means, feel free to scratch the ones you consider eye-roll worthy and highlight only the ones that lift you up. Even more! If you feel I left out important things, email me your suggestions. I will add them to future editions of the book and will give you credit in the acknowledgments.

But never, ever, allow shame or self-consciousness to get in the way of having a blast in life. What's more, don't ever waste your precious, short life worrying about what others will think of you. To close this chapter, allow me to quote one of my favorite fictional characters, T.J. Wagner, from my novel *Hope for Harmony*:

"I am not cool. I never was, never will be—and I'm not apologizing. The world doesn't need more people playing it cool—it's packed with them. (. . .) I'd rather laugh out loud than have a smug smile. I'd rather celebrate someone than burn them with wit and sarcasm. I'd rather be the one who makes people feel better about themselves. (. . .) *I don't want* to be cool. I'd rather be *warm.* (. . .) That's what I am! Warm and fuzzy, like your favorite plush sleepers or a cup of hot cocoa. Warm and cozy like that extra-soft blanket you snuggle under on the couch on a rainy night."

That speech is definitely me.

CONGRATULATIONS!

If you read this entire chapter (even the sections that don't apply to you), you just earned your advanced degree in joy. The last section of this book is the practical internship. It will focus on specific scenarios—life challenges—where you can apply this knowledge.

PART IV:
SPECIFIC SCENARIOS

G OOD NEWS! YOU'RE ALLOWED TO cherry-pick through the fourth part of this book. I do recommend you read the entire section, as every part will reinforce the learning process, but it's okay to read it out of order, skip parts that don't apply to you, and go straight to those you feel you need the most.

Here we'll be addressing challenges in five main categories:

1. Love life (heartbreak)

2. Human relationships (family and friends)

3. Career

4. Health

5. Loss of a loved one or facing death

As you read through the different topics, you will see both repetition and variation of the main techniques we've learned until now. In some cases, I'll refer to the seven-step formula to bounce back from acute problems (which I summarize as three steps, "This sucks—pick yourself up—let's find solutions"). In other moments I'll refer to the recipe to deal with chronic problems (Radical acceptance—mood vigilance—living in the now). In some cases, it will be both, as chronic issues often require extra help for acute exacerbations. In addition to those familiar concepts, I will also provide new tools and reframes for each area.

And, of course, if you need additional help, I'll be happy to work one-on-one with you to help you apply and individualize these strategies. For a complimentary session, please visit my website at www.joyfullysuccessful.com

Ready? Let's dive in.

19

HEARTBREAK, DIVORCE, AND THE END OF ROMANTIC RELATIONSHIPS

H EALING AND LEARNING FROM THE end of a romantic relationship is crucial before we're able to move on and, if we wish, find love again. But even if we eventually decide to remain single, the experience we acquired from a breakup can help us in all other non-romantic relationships for the rest of our lives. In addition to clarifying what we do and don't want, broken relationships point out old wounds we need to heal and behavior patterns hurting us and others.

In this chapter, I share a series of steps I took to speed up my recovery from the end of my previous marriage. I credit those for my rapid healing and the happiness I enjoy today with my husband.

THERE'S NO SUCH THING AS AN EASY DIVORCE

I won't dwell much on my former marriage. I'll just admit that I probably should've never married my ex in the first place. He was the first and only man I'd ever dated since age nineteen, and I agreed to marry him shortly after my mother died—a moment when I was unfit to make life-changing decisions. Soon, we were stuck in that type of soul-draining interaction where two human beings who are otherwise good separate bring the worst out in each other. Finalizing the divorce was a huge relief—and it *still* hurt. Even if we don't think we'll miss the other person, we're still facing the loss of a dream and the end of a stage of our lives.

When you part from a former partner, you need to allow yourself to say goodbye and grieve, which implies remembering *both the bad and the good*.

If we don't, we risk getting stuck either in unforgiveness or on idealizing the other person—both scenarios detrimental to our ability to rebuild our lives. Grieving is particularly important after divorce or the end of long relationships, when we're also leaving behind a chunk of our history—even losing friends and family.

The process of bouncing back from heartbreak follows a similar pattern we have used before when discussing acute setbacks: admitting "this sucks," picking yourself up, and then moving on. Here I share the exercises that helped me speed this process drastically at that time.

1. THE GOODBYE LETTER—(THE CLOSURE LETTER, HEARTBREAK VERSION)

I strongly recommend John Gray's book *Mars and Venus Starting Over*. In this book, he claims that to finish grieving, we must process *four* feelings: sadness, anger, fear, and regret. If we fail to process one of those feelings, we'll get stuck in one or more of the others. To those feelings, I dare to add that we also need to vent shame and guilt, if applicable.

In my case, before the end of my marriage, I spent years stuck in sadness, fear, and victim identity. Only when I tapped into my anger and allowed myself to process it could I finally move on.

The Goodbye Letter is a variant from the exercise at the end of Chapter 11. Here you'll write a letter to your former partner you don't intend to send.

GET YOUR JOURNAL AND GET COMFORTABLE

Start by journaling about your sadness. Did you decide to break the relationship? Vent about your broken dreams and disappointment. Did the other person decide against your will? Allow yourself to feel the abandonment and the blow to your self-esteem. Did you ever experience mistreatment or abuse in the relationship? Give yourself permission to feel like a victim for one last time. While venting sadness, explore if you feel any shame or guilt about giving up on the other person and "failing" the relationship. Cry if needed.

Then journal about the anger. Anger is usually the feeling we need to tap into to take action. Were you the person who broke up the relationship?

Then, you've probably been running resentments through your mind to give yourself the momentum to break up. Go on a rant. Complain about every senseless fight. Protest about every special or vulnerable moment your partner spoiled for you. Protest about every dream you gave up trying to please them. Protest about everything you ever did that went unappreciated.

Then process the fear. Did your partner ever lose his or her temper in a way that scared you? Were you ever afraid that your fights would escalate to physical violence—or perhaps they did? Did your partner ever snap or yell at you or your children in a way that left you raw and shaky? Or did you have to endure episodes of silent treatment or a cold shoulder in which you walked on eggshells, anticipating a backlash any minute? Do you currently fear you'll be unable to move on and rebuild your life?

After you're done with those feelings, acknowledge your regrets. Is there anything you still berate yourself for not doing differently? Do you regret the time lost? Giving up a dream? Do you regret losing your place in your ex's extended family? Losing your parents or siblings-in-law? Losing your dreams for a happy family together?

Keep in mind that, very often, we *especially* have to grieve *what we never had*. For example, I had once dreamed that my ex would be my source of support and strength when losing my mother and immigrating to a new country. In reality, he could never offer me that; he was just as broken and empty of resources as I was at the time. I had to admit that when I missed him, I was missing someone I never had.

A DRASTIC SWITCH IN GEARS

Take all the time you need on the Goodbye Letter, even if it implies taking breaks, putting the letter away, and returning the next day. But please push yourself to finish and move on to the next critical step, the one that will finally bring relief: After you've thoroughly vented those negative feelings, it's time to reconnect with *gratitude*.

This is the time to remember every single good thing that came into your life thanks to your ex, from children to fun dates, to trips together, to learning about a new band you wouldn't have discovered otherwise.

When I wrote my own letter, I cried tears of gratitude and sincerely thanked God for the years I had with my ex. He'd been there during my mother's health decline and death, even donating blood and coming to the house to start IVs. He'd been the main reason I came to the United States for medical training. He'd been all the family I had during those hard years of early training in Detroit. He'd given me my children. He'd been the influence that convinced me to stay in the United States after finishing training. My life would not be a sliver of what it was if it hadn't been for him. And I also thanked God and my ex for the small things. For example, he was the first person who introduced me to fancy, flavored coffee, Baskin Robbins ice cream, and the music of Phil Collins.

If you've done the previous steps without restraint, this moment should bring more bittersweetness than sadness. But it's okay to cry again if you feel like it.

TIME TO LET GO

The last step should feel like a wave of relief, but it might also be emotional. When you have run out of great memories to thank your ex for, then write your own version of the following sentences:

"Thank you again. Now, I wish you well and release you from my life. Today, I let you go."

Pro Tip: If you have any other past ex-partner that still brings out residual pain when you think of them, that means you haven't had full closure yet— even if you're sure you're over them and don't want them back. I encourage you also to write them a letter that you never intend to send. You can do this as many times as needed.

I've shared this exercise with many women over the years, and everyone reported miraculous results. Only one woman that I can remember decided to mail the letter for real. You decide what you want to do with that letter. Instead of mailing it, you might want to get rid of it in a symbolic way that represents your releasing the ex from your life (burning the letter, or ripping it apart and throwing the pieces in the ocean or a strong wind). You might even consider combining that moment of getting rid of the letter with one of the two following tools: The Funeral and Release Ceremonies.

Please note: The Goodbye Letter is the most important tool in this chapter and the one that will have the biggest effect on your ability to move on. If you can only do one step, do this one. However, I believe in consolidating ideas and sending the brain crystal-clear messages. The next two steps, the Funeral and the Release Ceremony, will enhance the process of the Goodbye Letter and help reinforce your feeling of closure and freedom.

2. THE FUNERAL

The funeral ceremony is an example of inducing catharsis. You might choose to do it at the same time you write the Goodbye Letter or *before it* if you still don't feel ready to let go, or if you're having trouble accessing the feelings to vent.

I came up with this idea at the end of my divorce process. I'd been separated from my ex for almost two years. Still, the day the divorce became final felt like pulling the plug on a loved one who'd been brain dead for months. Even if that person wasn't truly alive any longer and pulling the plug was just a bureaucratic step, I knew it would stir strong emotions inside. I was afraid grief would hit me when least expected, and I would lose it in front of my children. So, to avoid that, I *scheduled* time to cry and vent away from my kids and decided to make it a "funeral" for my marriage.

On the day of my divorce hearing, I took the afternoon off from work, left the kids with the sitter, and locked myself in my hiding place—an empty apartment I owned as a rental property. There, I played a mixed CD I'd once made for our anniversary (today, it would be a playlist). The CD included a collection of songs that made the soundtrack of that relationship. From Jon Secada's hit "Angel," which came out when we first started dating, to Kenny Rogers' "Through the Years," the song my ex had requested to play during our wedding. That day I did the Goodbye Letter one last time, unburying even more memories and grieving them. I cried and journaled passionately. Knowing the marriage was officially over opened a new set of fears—fears of never finding love again and the fears of making the same mistakes in a future relationship.

Then, when the time was up, I washed my face, reapplied my makeup, and went home to the kids feeling a thousand pounds lighter.

Pro Tip: Doing the Goodbye Letter at the same time as the funeral offers the advantage of putting a time limit to how long you'll spend on your letter. That decreases the chances of getting stuck in bad memories.

Then, if you really, really want to take your closure to the next level, consider adding one last step: The Release Ceremony.

3. A RELEASE CEREMONY

Some of my friends found the next tip fascinating, while others cringed at it. But anyone who decided to try it out later reported dramatic improvement in their inner peace and ability to move on.

The Release Ceremony takes the process of closure to yet another level. In this exercise, you plan a symbolic act (or acts) that will represent your decision to let go of this stage of your life. To get the best out of it, set a date and time in your calendar so you can prepare mentally for a few days. It could be something you do instead of the funeral, immediately after it, or a few days later. You might choose to do this alone or with one or more friends as witnesses. Surrounding yourself with comforting people will make it easier and more official.

Examples of symbolic actions include:

1. Tearing up your Goodbye Letter and releasing the pieces in the wind while saying a prayer.

2. Burning the photographs, love letters, or cards you were still holding on to while singing a song you associate with your ending relationship.

3. Throwing an object symbolic of the time with your ex in the ocean.

In addition to choosing a date/time and an act, it might get your inspiration going if you think about a *meaningful theme*. Examples of themes would be:

1. Military honors: We're saying goodbye to someone who had a sad ending but will be forever be remembered for giving their life for a greater cause.

2. Spiritual/Magic ceremony: Time it with the full moon. Burn incense or sage. Sprinkle blessed water. Say a prayer.

3. Sensorial pleasures theme: Add music you love. Include in the ceremony anything that puts you in a blissful mood—from aromatherapy to wind chimes.

Your imagination is the limit, and you decide how short or long you need this ceremony to be. Just make sure that before or after it, you can have a moment of peaceful introspection. As usual, whatever you choose has to feel right to you.

My own Release Ceremony was probably a bigger production than you need, but I'll share it anyway to get your ideas jumpstarted:

MY RELEASE CEREMONY

A few days after the funeral I held for my deceased marriage, I had a Release Ceremony at the beach. I got the idea from a book about shamanic ceremonies I'd just read. The book claimed that the sunset was the time of the day that represented endings, and the full moon the time of the month to symbolize completion, so I chose both.

I invited a handful of my best friends to come with me to the beach at sunset, a full moon night. With me, I brought a handful of objects tied to my past. My diamond wedding ring; some of my wedding pictures; the very first present my ex gave me, a tiny seashell box; and the last wedding present I had kept, a wooden decorative cross that hung on my bedroom wall for years.

There, I read aloud some lines I'd written about saying goodbye to an era of my life and starting a new one. I handed the diamond wedding ring to one of my friends to donate to her cancer foundation, as a symbol of what I was letting go of. I took the much more humble present my ex had given me, the seashell box, expressed my gratitude and love for it, and kept it as a symbol of the good memories that will always be with me.

Then came a step I compare to the burial or cremation after the funeral. I burned my Goodbye Letter along with the wedding pictures. My original plan was to release the ashes in the wind, but not wanting to poison any sea life, I changed plans there. Instead, I decided to dig "a grave" and bury them in the sand to rest forever.

Then, I took one last symbolic action of my liberation from the past by throwing the wooden cross, my only surviving wedding gift, into the ocean. After so many steps, you would think that one was unnecessary, but I can't begin to describe the immense relief I felt at that moment. I'd once said that my ex was "my cross to carry." Now, I was exercising my power of free will, giving God that cross back, and He was willingly taking it away from me. I was ready to see the next relationship in my life, not as a cross but as a blessing.

In your case, whatever act you choose should be meaningful to *you*.

I AGREE. I OVERDID IT

Granted, you may not need all three steps. You can always pick and choose one or more, and obviously, you should only do what deeply resonates with you.

But I did all three and can give testimony that my results were amazing. I immediately felt a release of energy previously holding me back. And it was a matter of months until I met my new husband, David. I firmly believe that the "lightness in my soul" those steps generated allowed me to be in the receiving mode and open when he came into my life.

AFTER CLOSURE COMES THE MOST IMPORTANT PART: FIND THE LESSONS LEARNED

After these steps, make sure to *return to gratitude*. This step is vital no matter which of the three previous techniques you used to reconnect with your feelings. To begin picking yourself up, you must determine what you learned from the experience.

Sit down and evaluate (preferably in writing) what you learned from this relationship and what you need to do differently in the next one.

In my case, the first one was "choosing better." No amount of work on a relationship will be able to save it if it started for the wrong reasons, like in my case. I promised myself that the next time I chose to enter a romantic relationship, I would do it only for someone I was crazy about—truly loved, admired, and respected.

I invite you to do the same. In which ways did you suspect early on that your former partner was not right for you? Were there any red flags you ignored? What do you want in your next relationship?

But beyond that, own your part in the breakup. In my case, I admitted that I came to the relationship with horribly low self-esteem. Most offenses I'd taken from my ex were actually echoes of my own self-berating voices.

Nothing he ever said to me was more hurting than what I was telling myself every day.

Also, I had to own my inability to set boundaries. I was desperate to please and gave, gave, and gave, but never thought about asking clearly for what I needed—something that invariably leads to resentment. I didn't know yet how to use my voice, so I swung in a pendulum of obedient submission and rebellion.

I'm glad to report that learning all that has made a huge difference in my second marriage. And looking back, the path to my current happiness resembles an amazingly written plot. If it hadn't been for my ex, I would've never heard of the city of Melbourne, Florida, and would've never met my soulmate, my husband, David.

A DIFFERENT VERSION OF HEARTBREAK: CHRONIC DISSATISFACTION

Being chronically stuck in an unsatisfactory relationship hurts less in the short-term than having one's heart broken—but it costs us more in the long-term. If that is your case, I encourage you to go back to Chapter 13 and read the section "Chronic Dissatisfaction." As a reminder, the steps to follow center around the chronic issues triad: Radical acceptance, mood vigilance, and living in the now. I encourage you to use the Truth Serum tool to admit why you are unhappy in your relationship and own your part. Then, I invite you to get clear on what you want and the type of person you need to become to attract that type of relationship in your life.

Seeking this clarity can transform your life in one of two opposite ways. You might discover what needs to improve in your current relationship so it matches your ideal—or it'll become clearer that it's time to end it.

IN SUMMARY

There's no shortcut for healing from heartbreak. In order to move on and maximize our chances of finding love again, we must grieve and learn from the experience.

20
RELATIONSHIP CHALLENGES AND FAMILY FEUDS

A S WE BEGIN THIS CHAPTER, let's get a tricky subject out of the way: Yes, sometimes you have to "divorce" a family member (an abusive parent, a toxic sibling, an adult child who keeps betraying your trust). Sometimes, after you've done your best to preserve the relationship, you arrive at the painful conclusion that your only chance to help them is to practice tough love—withdrawing from their lives. I compare it to saying, "I love you, but I can't continue to enable you. I can't allow you to drag me down with you." If that has been the case in your life, the closure tools in the previous chapter on heartbreak and divorce will help you tremendously.

But let's face it; firing a relative from our lives is an option we should reserve for extreme cases. Luckily, if we just hang in there and don't give up, most of our conflicts with loved ones can be resolved. In fact, part of our growth process involves navigating those disagreements successfully.

All the tools we've discussed so far will help you weather relationship challenges. Some of those issues will be acute and require the use of the tools for acute problems—for example, recovering your good mood after your son gets in trouble at school. In other moments, you'll need to tap into the chronic tools, such as navigating a demanding, aging parent. Often, you'll need to use both—like when your chronically tense relationship with your sister worsens after a loud argument at the Thanksgiving table.

In this chapter, we'll refresh the previous strategies and how they apply to human relationships.

THE MINDSET TRIAD:
SELF-COMPASSION, PERSPECTIVE, AND WILLINGNESS
TO LEARN FROM THE EXPERIENCE (SEE CHAPTER 9)

SELF-COMPASSION

Often, people in conflict with us resort to personal attacks, guilt-tripping, or hashing over previous mistakes to make us doubt ourselves. The closer to home those attacks touch, the more defensive we get and the more we attack back. If we can forgive ourselves for the mistakes made, attacks become much less likely to get us off-center, and it decreases the intensity of the vicious cycle.

Example: My oldest son soon learned to guilt me, saying, "You don't really care for me." As a teenager, he'd back this up with "evidence," pointing out that over the years, I'd missed most of his after-school games. As a busy working mother, that argument never failed to make me feel guilty. If I allowed myself to fall into self-shame, the argument would spiral down from there.

Learning to neutralize those attacks took some work on self-compassion. After those fights, I would journal or meditate, recounting all the evidence I had that I did love him. I remembered all those times I played with him, kissed his booboos, or faked a visit from Santa or the tooth fairy. And yes, I listed all the times I did make it to the after-school activities, rushing straight from work despite my fatigue. The moment I remembered that his words were false, they had much less power to hurt me. The next time he'd accused me of not caring for him, I'd be ready to smile with sincere love and say, "You're talking nonsense, and you know it."

PERSPECTIVE

The next mindset is perspective. So much of what upsets us about our loved ones would shrink drastically if we stopped to think for a moment. Really? Here I am getting irritated because my husband is slurping his soup or my kid left a mess in the bathroom? I have in front of me an amazing human being, full of wonderful qualities and even idiosyncrasies I love—and I'm going to get stuck on this one little thing?

Believe it or not, there's someone out there who wishes they had your problems. Are you clashing with your son, like I was in my last personal example? Well, there's someone somewhere in the world who dreamed of having children and didn't and would gladly take an argumentative teenage son if it meant they could experience parenthood. Do you fight with your husband? There are plenty of women out there who wish they had a husband to quarrel with. The same goes if you're clashing with a sibling or a friend.

For example, many of my friends are currently dealing with elderly, declining mothers suffering from dementia and health issues. I can feel their pain and exhaustion as they grieve the younger, stronger mother they used to have. I got a small taste of that with my father-in-law, Del. And yes, it's soul-draining. I don't attempt to minimize how difficult that process is, but to my friends, I sincerely tell them, "I wish I had your problem."

I mean it. My mother died from cancer at age fifty-one. She never got to meet her grandchildren—which was her lifelong dream. I couldn't have her there with me the day of my wedding. I missed her terribly during my pregnancies when I had to give birth without anyone to hold my hand and answer my questions about newborn care. If God, or a fairy godmother, or an alien with a quantum time machine said, "I have a deal for you. We'll go back in time, change the past, and you will have a mother for those two or three decades you got cheated of. But there's a price. You will have to deal with her being elderly and demented at the end of her life." Do you know what I would answer?

"YES, PLEASE! Bring it on!"

AND NEVER FORGET: IT COULD'VE ALWAYS BEEN WORSE, MUCH WORSE.

Do you remember the exercise about having fun with catastrophic thinking? You can add a twist of perspective to any conflict if you remember that it could've always been worse. Yes, that manipulative mother might be a drag—but at least she had you instead of aborting you. Yes, that father with alcoholic tendencies is painful to deal with—but at least he didn't murder you at age five.

In a simpler version of exercising perspective, my friend Belle has a go-to phrase she tells herself when she's getting upset about small stuff her children or husband are doing. She throws her hands in the air and exclaims, "First World country problems!" She explained it to me once, saying, "I remind myself that somewhere in Ethiopia there's a village starving—and here I am upset about my husband or one of my kids stealing my cell phone charger."

WILLINGNESS TO LEARN FROM THE EXPERIENCE:

People from very different backgrounds have shared a crazy but very interesting idea: "We choose our relatives before our birth."

I've heard people who believe in reincarnation say the same souls travel together and make covenants to support each other life after life. I've also heard people from more conservative religious backgrounds who *don't* believe in reincarnation say before our souls enter our pre-birth bodies, God gives us a chance to choose the people who will be our parents, our siblings, our neighbors. It's all pre-planned to allow the maximum possible spiritual growth.

I've always found the idea fascinating, and it certainly seems plausible. More than once, I witnessed my babies light up with joy at the sight of their grandpa Diego, my father—even if they'd never seen him before or only seen him once as newborns. Were they reacting to some DNA message? Or was it recognition from the soul level? Could it be true that we're here in each other's lives for a reason, and we chose each other as travel companions eternities ago?

If you don't subscribe to the belief that we have a pre-birth or after-death life, I encourage you to play with the idea for a moment from a more scientific angle. Even secular psychology acknowledges that we tend to choose friends and romantic partners who push our buttons in the same way that our parents or siblings did—it's our way to heal our unfinished businesses from childhood. For example, the shy and quiet woman marries an overbearing, loud man who reminds her unconsciously of her mother. Without knowing it, she seeks to recreate the conditions that hurt her in the past so that she can give them a different ending now. Every time that husband annoys her with his excessive talking, she has an opportunity to break her fear, assert herself, and fight for the right of speaking out. Also, by living with people who are very different from us and who have overdeveloped personality traits we haven't developed, we are forced to stretch ourselves and become more balanced individuals.

So, holding that idea in our mind, I extend a challenge to you. Every time someone in your inner circle pushes your buttons, say quietly, "Thank you for the opportunity to learn something new about myself." Then grab your journal afterward and ask yourself some questions:

What exactly did they do or say that hurt you?

Is this a repetitive pattern?

Is this related to one of your original wounds from childhood?

How have you reacted in the past, and how can you act differently in the future?

And most importantly: What is the trait you're being called to develop to give the story a different ending?

A personal example: Since childhood, I had suffered from a desperate need for approval from parents and teachers. I vowed exemplary behavior, compulsively sought academic awards, and sacrificed my early social life on behalf of getting straight As. Coincidence or unconscious drive, I ended up marrying my ex—someone impossible to please.

Longing for my ex-husband's praise, I took note of his wishes and did everything I could to impress him—from buying him his dream birthday presents to learning to cook his favorite dinners (and God knows housewife skills are not my strength). On a good day, he didn't even notice; on bad days, he'd tear apart what I did, pinpointing every tiny mistake. I constantly felt like a failure.

I learned an important lesson through all this, which helped me tremendously in my current, happy marriage. The solution wasn't to try harder the next time, hoping to succeed at pleasing. Instead, I learned not to measure myself against someone else's standard. I was already the harshest judge of everything I did. I strived for excellence in every task I performed. I had to remember that, acknowledge myself for doing my best, and not expect others to reassure me.

Yes, it helps being married to someone who does appreciate my efforts (another lesson learned). But nowadays, if I don't feel I'm being appreciated enough for something, I'm able to just smile at David and joke, "Hey, Honey, this is the part when you're supposed to say, 'Great job, wonderful wife!'"

BOUNCING BACK FROM ACUTE CLASHES:

Even the best of relationships endures disagreements and disappointments. You know. *Problems*. I will classify relationship problems as *acute* when they are new, sudden, and usually time-limited. They can be big or small, but at the time, they feel sharply painful because they destabilize us. If we deal well with them, they can be solved completely without scars and even move the relationship forward. But if poorly managed, they can become chronic issues, lead to chronic dissatisfaction and damage the relationship. Examples of acute problems in relationships would be:

- A fight because your spouse said something that hurt your feelings.

- Your teenager is caught drinking at a party.

- You get locked in a dead-end disagreement about politics with a relative you usually get along with.

The tools we'll be reviewing in this section are the ones we introduced in Chapter 12. In addition to helping with acute setbacks, they'll also help you when you face acute exacerbations of chronic issues. That is, when a problem that has been dragging for a while suddenly worsens. Examples of acute exacerbations of chronic issues include:

- The spouse you're always unhappy with forgets your birthday.

- The teenager with a habitual drug problem has a relapse.

- The sibling with whom you have a strained relationship makes a life decision you strongly disagree with.

To refresh your memory, there are seven steps we follow when bouncing back from an acute setback. These are:

1. Breathing through the waves.

2. Grounding yourself in the storm.

3. Engaging in mindless (not brainless) activity.

4. Remembering perspective and gratitude.

5. Finding the lessons to be learned.

6. Lifting your spirits while staying in the now.

7. Looking for solutions.

If recalling seven steps is difficult, remember the shortcut three steps 1-This sucks. 2-Picking yourself up. 3-Searching for solutions.

STEP 1: THIS SUCKS—BUT IT WON'T KILL ME

When in the middle of a fight with a loved one, or when facing heart-rending disappointment, it's easy to give into instinctive rage or despair and think there's no hope for the relationship. Remind yourself that, contrary to physical pain, emotional pain won't kill you. The more comfortable you get with discomfort, the quicker you'll bounce back the next time.

Avoid numbing yourself. At this early stage, it's critical to allow yourself to feel your sadness, anger, hurt, and disappointment. Don't shame yourself for them, and don't rush them. Otherwise, you risk that unprocessed feelings may become future resentments.

A tool that has been particularly helpful for me is the *Truth Serum*. (See Chapter 11). On the rare occasions when my husband, David, and I have a disagreement that escalates into a fight, I make an entry in my journal that starts with: "The truth, the whole truth, and nothing but the truth." (Or TTTWTANBT). Onto the page, I pour my anger, hurt, or dissatisfaction with the situation. But I also acknowledge my part in it and notice when I'm overreacting. By the time I'm done venting, the intensity of the feelings has deflated so much that I can talk to him calmly, *asking for what I need from him* instead of complaining. But more often than not, the exercise allows me to see things differently and realize there was no reason to be upset to begin with.

You'll be ready to crawl out of your dark mood once you find an anchor to hold on to or a patch of solid ground to stand on. That can be the love you feel for that person or one of your values, such as the sacredness of family.

STEP 2: PICKING YOURSELF UP

Make sure to keep an eye on your Feelings Thermostat (see Chapter 2). A negative or very low positive score for joy suggests you're not done venting. Once you see the needle moving up to a positive 4 or higher, dive into your list of preferred joy activities to boost that joy number. I recommend resisting the temptation to go straight to Mind Candy and instead start with mindless activity or something productive. Cleaning your kitchen, organizing your closet, or folding laundry will reassure your brain that you're not powerless. Adjust your Feelings Thermostat as needed through enjoyable music, people, and pleasant tasks.

Make sure you've returned to at least a positive 6-7 joy score before you attempt to look into solutions.

STEP 3: FINDING SOLUTIONS

With a more positive attitude, this is the moment to find solutions or start diplomatic efforts anchored in your values. I strongly recommend creating a positive intention for the relationship. More than saying, "I want my husband to stop drinking," or "I want my teenager to listen," or "I want my brother to stop behaving like an idiot," we go much deeper to connect with the feelings we want to experience.

Examples of relationship intentions are:

"I enjoy a mutually respectful and deeply loving relationship with my husband. I support him in improving his health."

"I relish seeing my son grow into a happy, successful, integral man who finds fulfillment while contributing to society."

"I enjoy a loving connection with my brother based on what joins us, instead of what separates us—a relationship solid enough that allows us to speak our truths while respecting each other's opinions."

When you've written a positive intention that resonates with your dream scenario, you can make it the relationship *mission statement*. Return to it in the future when you need a reminder of what's important.

CHRONIC RELATIONSHIP CHALLENGES

Chronic issues require the same mindset we opened with but demand a different set of tools and skills we can use in the long run. This is the triad: Radical acceptance, Mood vigilance, Staying in the now (see Chapter 13).

RADICAL ACCEPTANCE

In his book *The Mastery of Love,* Don Miguel Ruiz compares our unrealistic expectations about our loved ones to owning a pet. It would be absurd to have a dog and want it to become a cat. Either you love and accept your pets for what they are, or you don't—but you don't attempt to make them into something they're not. It's the same with our spouses, relatives, and friends. We relieve much of our suffering when we admit our loved ones are who they are, and we'll never make them change.

In the same way, we'll often have to practice radical acceptance of situations that may or may not ever change. Our ability to help a spouse with a drinking problem or a son who struggles at school because of ADHD starts by embracing the situation as is, no longer denying or resisting it. (I discuss chronic health issues like these in Chapter 22).

MOOD VIGILANCE

When dealing with chronic dissatisfaction, it's more important than ever to stick to your Joy Diet (daily doses of joy-generating activities). Remember to check your Thermostat regularly and adjust it through extra joy activities, aiming to keep it at positive 7-9.

If you need an additional refresher for this, please refer to Chapters 2 to 7.

STAYING IN THE NOW

When dealing with strained relationships, we tend to carry the baggage of all previous conflicts to every interaction we have—and that's a mistake. In a perfect world, we would fully process each issue as it happens and face each new problem with a clean slate. Like a couples therapist I once met said, "Get the trash out every day, so it doesn't accumulate." And also, "If it happened more than two weeks ago, it's ancient history and should not be mentioned." Those two pieces of advice have worked wonders in my life.

If you have some catching up to do from hurts from the past, I strongly recommend the Closure Letter tool. In that exercise, you write a venting letter to that particular person—a letter you never intend to send. In it, you tell them everything you wished you'd told them at the time and process your sadness, anger, fear, regrets, shame, and guilt. Then when you're done, end with gratitude—thank them for the lessons learned, and commit to leaving that grudge in the past.

IN SUMMARY

When our relationships are going right, they can definitely be our biggest source of joy, support, and sense of belonging. When they're going wrong, they become an opportunity for us to grow and deepen our self-awareness. If we root ourselves in perspective, we'll see that even having someone to fight with is already a blessing not everyone enjoys. The key to fulfilling relationships is gratitude and staying in the now without carrying old grudges. This is much easier to achieve if we take the time to process day-to-day hurts and radically accept our loved ones for who they are.

21
CAREER SETBACKS

THE LAST CHAPTER OF MY CAREER CRISIS STORY

REMEMBER THE FIRST TWO CHAPTERS of my career saga? I'd become a hematologist-oncologist because I needed to grieve my mother—not the healthiest reason. I'd entered my practice with outstanding training and a great set of social skills—compassion, empathy, and a personal investment in the fight against cancer. But I didn't realize at the time those skillsets were not an asset but a handicap. Precisely because of them, I lacked the most important skill an oncologist needs: the ability to disconnect from the patient's suffering.

Again and again, I fell in love with my new patients and became too invested in their treatment process. Even in the best-case scenario, when they were cured of their cancers, I felt as if I were keeping them alive with my sheer mental power. By the end of their treatments, I felt exhausted, as if I'd given each one of them a transfusion of my own blood.

Then, of course, there was the worst-case scenario, witnessing patients die. Powerless to rescue them, I watched them decline and extinguish in front of my eyes, an endless repetition of my mother's story. And the worst part, I didn't have time to slow down, process the loss, and grieve. Because for every patient who lost the battle, I had a dozen more who needed my attention to keep going. If I managed to encase myself in a hard shell, it was worse. Attempting to treat patients from an emotional distance only removed the reward of human connection and highlighted the job's meaningless bureaucracy.

I spent years pushing myself through the burnout, desperately trying to make it work. Quitting oncology would've been betraying my mother's memory, admitting that her suffering and death had been in vain. Let alone all the practical reasons why I would be crazy to quit—a huge income and excellent benefits. And what about the investment I'd made so far? To become an oncologist, I'd sacrificed over a decade of my life between medical school, residency, and fellowship. My whole identity was tied to "Dr. Pichardo, a Board-Certified Hematologist-Oncologist."

Yet, I'd reached a point of feeling literally nauseous every Sunday evening, just remembering I had to return to work.

WHEN IT RAINS, IT POURS

My mother used to say, "When God touches you with His right hand, listen—so He doesn't have to smack you with His left hand."

Whether coincidence or consequence of my inner dissonance, the number of patients referred to my medical group dropped—and I felt secretly relieved. While my business partners considered a full waiting room a sign of practice well-being, I saw it as a depressing reminder of the explosion of cancer statistics. No wonder I dreaded marketing my practice. My efforts to gain more referrals were half-hearted at best.

But the drop in patients also caused a drop in revenue for the clinic. Combined with how outrageously expensive chemotherapy drugs had become, within months, the practice fell into the red by hundreds of thousands of dollars. To save the practice, my business partner and I had to repay the deficit. And to cut the only expense we could control, we had to stop collecting a salary for at least six months.

Now I had not only the most painful job in the world—I had to do it without a paycheck.

THE WAY OUT IS A JOURNEY INWARD

I know leaving a painful career is possible because I did it. But precisely because I've been there, I'm aware that when we're stuck in an undesirable situation, we don't see a way out. We convince ourselves that we won't be able to find work soon enough to survive financially. We talk ourselves into thinking we should be glad we at least have a job. Even more, we convince ourselves that our suffering is worth it because we're enduring it for the love of our families—so the people we support can have a good life. It took me years to realize my unhappiness at my job permeated my family life and deeply hurt my husband and children.

How did I manage to escape the dead-end career situation I'd placed myself in? To answer that question, let's refresh some of the concepts we've learned and apply them to this scenario.

The previous story exemplifies a chronic career issue (my burnout) that became exacerbated by an acute event (learning I would not be collecting a salary for months). Acute career challenges materialize as a sudden, unexpected blow, while more pervasive chronic issues happen over a longer time. The worst version of chronic career issues is chronic career dissatisfaction—or low-grade misery. Things aren't bad enough to quit— but deep inside, you know you want more.

We'll start with the "easy" part first: Acute challenges.

ACUTE CAREER ISSUES

The most obvious example of an acute career issue is losing your job. Other examples include being demoted, getting a salary reduction, or being transferred to a less pleasant department. By definition, acute problems are time-limited. If we just hang in there for long enough, things will settle again—or we'll adapt.

Managing those acute issues well is critical so they don't become a chronic problem. To deal with them, I encourage you to apply the seven steps in Chapter 12, "Bouncing back in one-two-three."

These are:

1. Breathing through the waves.

2. Grounding yourself in the storm.

3. Engaging in mindless (not brainless) activity.

4. Remembering perspective and gratitude.

5. Finding the lessons to be learned.

6. Lifting your spirits while staying in the now.

7. Looking for solutions.

If recalling seven steps is difficult, remember the shortcut three steps 1-This sucks. 2-Picking yourself up. 3-Searching for solutions. In summary: accept that the situation is undesirable (take your time processing the feelings), then work on raising your spirits before making a decision in alignment with your core values. This will be particularly important if your decision implies quitting your job and finding a new one. I encourage you to review Chapter 12 if you need a refresher on these steps and on how to create an intention and a goal for your next life chapter.

Acute career challenges are deeply painful at the time, but they can provide a great opportunity for a new beginning. Chronic issues, on the other hand, can be the most challenging because as we adapt to them, our drive to leave is hampered. Let's explore them in more detail.

CHRONIC CAREER ISSUES

Warning. I'm about to say something controversial that will make many people wince.

Career issues only become chronic if we have a mental block that prevents us from seeking happiness.

Look at it like this: career issues are different from other topics we've discussed here in that we do ultimately have control over them. I couldn't "fire" my cancer diagnosis or "quit" being the caregiver of a child with special needs, at least not without betraying my core values. But I could've decided to step out from my painful career at any time—and so can you. What took me so long?

Yes, I had real ties that stopped me from making an impulsive decision—for example, a financial penalty for early contract termination and a restriction covenant, a clause that forbade me from practicing oncology in my city after my exit. However, the biggest blocks arose from *inside* me, a collection of beliefs that came from growing up in a Third World country and hearing my parents say, "Just look at the poverty around you. You have no right to complain." It came from a scarcity mentality whispering in my brain, "If you leave this job—this career—you'll never find another one." And it came from a recurring tendency to lose contact with my inner voice on behalf of a greater cause.

If you've been feeling miserable in your job for a while, yet have taken no steps toward leaving, I encourage you to explore the reason. Ask yourself: "Why am I putting up with mistreatment or misery without drawing a firm boundary? Do I doubt that I deserve better? Am I failing to value myself also in other areas of my life?"

Even more, I encourage you to speak the absolute truth and ask yourself if you have any blocks against a fully realized life: "Do I really—really—want to be happy? Do I think I have dues to pay or guilt to expiate by being here? Has this unhappiness become my identity? Am I addicted to complaining? Is being stuck in an unhappy job situation my way to avoid confronting a more serious life decision?" To expand on those topics, I encourage you to review Chapter 16, Troubleshooting 101.

BECOMING UNSTUCK FROM CHRONIC JOB DISSATISFACTION

STEP 1: SPEAK THE TRUTH TO YOURSELF

We'll only be able to move on when we reach a tilting point—when the weight of our unhappiness with a situation outbalances the rewards we're getting from it. The first step in any career decision will be to make a clear and sincere inventory of where we stand. Here I recommend the tool of the Truth Serum (Chapter 2). Remove all filters, avoid lies of omission, and make a written account of how you really feel. Long before we're ready to try something new, we need to get emotionally unstuck from the old. If needed, use the outline of the Closure Letter (Chapter 11) to express your sadness, anger, fear, and regrets about your job.

STEP 2: CLARIFY WHAT YOU WANT

The topic of how to reinvent a professional life is too extensive to cover in this book. If you're considering switching *careers,* you'll eventually need to spend some time clarifying your passions, aptitudes, and strengths and perhaps resort to vocational tests. But whether you're considering a drastic change or just a new job in the same field, the first step will be clarifying *exactly* what you want.

1.   Start by making a list of everything you dislike about your current situation. List every detail that enrages you, annoys you, or that

brings you cognitive dissonance. Be as specific as possible. Don't just write, "My boss is an idiot"; write exactly what it is that he or she does that upsets you. "My boss fixates on my mistakes and doesn't appreciate what I do right."

2. Then, when you're done, convert all those statements into positive ones to determine what you want.

   For example, if you wrote, "I hate that my boss fixates on my mistakes and doesn't appreciate what I do right." Then convert it to: "I want to work for someone who values me and appreciates my work."

3. Review your positive list and see what else you can add. Be specific in what you want, including salary, benefits, time off, and type of colleagues. This is dream mode, so include even how much freedom you would want and how much supervision (or not) you need from mentors. Imagine what a new career or ideal job would feel like.

STEP 3: TAKE RESPONSIBILITY

After you've described what you want in detail, ask yourself, "Who do I have to become to get a job like that?" The answer might come in the form of some training you need to take, or it may come as a new character trait you need to develop—such as self-confidence. Reflecting on your skills and character may also make you evaluate whether, at any point, you failed to give your best at your work or made mistakes in your interactions with others.

I encourage you to go back to Chapter 13 and read the section on chronic dissatisfaction to expand on the concepts in steps 2 and 3.

STEP 4: FACE YOUR INNER CONFLICT

By now, you might've already noticed the contradictory voices inside you.

"I want more money—but I don't want to have to work more hours."

"I want a job that gives me more executive power—but I don't want to become a workaholic who never sees her family."

"I want freedom—but I also need supervision."

These seemingly contradictory statements are often the source of our hesitation to quit our current job.

More often than not, bringing those fears to the surface weakens their power. You can unearth those worries by talking to a friend about them. But I encourage you to take it one step further: Have a *conversation* with all the different conflicting voices inside you. Grab your journal, listen to each one of them give their opinions, and write them as dialogue. Can you envision all these voices as different members of a team having an executive meeting? Can you name the stronger voices, reason with them, and call for compromises and agreements? Is there any part of you that needs reassurance that any decision you take will be in agreement with your innermost values? I did this with the help of hypnotherapy, and it helped me restore inner coherence. Nowadays, I need no more help than my journal and a willingness to pay attention to my inner dialogue.

STEP 5: COMMIT TO MOOD MANAGING.

Until you find your next job or career, don't place your life on hold; commit to enjoy each day and make the best out of the work you currently do.

Use all the tools in this book to regularly check your Mood Thermostat and then practice old and new joy-generating activities to keep your joy scores in the 7-9 range. Find other sources of satisfaction in your life to compensate for what your job is not giving you. Everything you wrote in your previous list that you want to receive from bosses and colleagues (appreciation, praise, approval) give to yourself and notice and be thankful when someone else gives it to you. Even more: *give it sincerely to others.* Regardless of whether you subscribe to the belief that your inner world affects your outer world, joyfulness will transform the way you present to others and make you a much more attractive candidate for whatever new position you eventually pursue.

In summary: By following the previous steps, you're more likely to notice opportunities around and break the paralysis of indecision. I also believe that when we mind our mood, know exactly what we want, and stop sending mixed signals, we immediately start moving the gadgets of the Universe to help us get it.

THE CONCLUSION OF MY CAREER CRISIS. SOMETIMES, WE HAVE TO TOUCH BOTTOM BEFORE WE CAN RESURFACE

While working with no salary for seven months proved to be one of the most stressful challenges I've ever faced, it was also a blessing in disguise. It pushed me to take a harsh look at my work and admit that, once I took money out of the equation, I had little left worth staying for. Oncology was no longer that calling I would've done for free. I'd begun to plan my exit when the cancer diagnosis, which I suspect was related to that chronic stress, delayed my plans.

Do you remember the third step of the Mindset Triad, "Willingness to learn from the experience?" I'm a firm believer that a seed of goodness hides even in the worst circumstances. I initially assumed that my cancer treatment would rescue my commitment to oncology. Instead, it opened my eyes to painful truths I'd been avoiding. The experience showed me the bad side effects of chemotherapy—worse than I'd convinced myself they were. It removed my denial about how terrifying the possibility of death is. And it showed me how clueless conventional medicine can often be to the true needs of a patient. Thanks to that bottom-touching experience and the hypnotherapy session I described previously, I was able to reconnect with my grief and process it, so I no longer had to punish myself with a job that caused me daily pain.

Then, I could follow the same steps I gave you earlier and declare, "I don't want to make a living anymore in a career that is based on sickness, suffering, and death. I don't want to meet people when it might be too late to make a difference in their lives." That became translated to. "I want to make a living spreading joy. I want to help others find the life purpose that I believe can induce true health. I want to reach people when they still have a chance to pursue passions and have the life of their dreams. I want to help others make the best out of the time they have left on this planet—no matter how short or long that might be."

That's how I feel every day when I work with Life Coaching clients and write books like this. Trust me—it's worth any moment of terror and indecision that lead to taking the jump. I wake up every morning looking forward to my day. And I feel more confident than ever about my own health. I feel my cells heal and regenerate every time I see the joy in the eyes of someone I helped.

CONCLUSION

Life is too short to postpone happiness. Please, don't wait until you're diagnosed with a terrible condition or until something in your life collapses and you touch bottom. Commit to finding a career in which you can truly feel you're contributing to the world in a way that resonates with your true self. Make a decision *today* that you will not settle for less than that.

22
HEALTH CHALLENGES

LIVING WITH A CHRONIC ILLNESS (FROM CANCER TO HEART DISEASE TO ALCOHOLISM)

I HAVE A MEMOIR IN DRAFT, talking about the irony of being a cancer specialist and becoming a cancer patient. Remembering my deeply set denial still makes me smile. Given my mother's history, I knew I carried a risk of having inherited some cancer gene, but I would've expected anything but breast cancer. Come on! I knew all the risk factors, and I had none of them. I was too young for that diagnosis. I had four children, and I'd started having them in my twenties. I'd breastfed them all. I'd never smoked in my life. I'd barely tasted alcohol. I'd always kept a healthy weight.

So that afternoon, when I walked out of the mammogram suite with an appointment for a biopsy, I felt absolutely convinced it would be negative.

It wasn't.

I barely remember the anger stage, which I shot toward the innocent (or not-so-innocent) bystanders at my work. I went through little sadness at first. Then, I got stuck in bargaining. I prayed and begged God to keep me alive through this because this experience would make me be a better oncologist. I also negotiated. "If I put up well with chemotherapy, I'll be able to give hope to my patients."

But even if I remained a strong pillar of support for my family like my mother had been, my true peace and healing didn't start until the day I allowed myself to take in the bad news and admit, "This sucks."

My oncologist happened to be my business partner, so the doctor-patient boundaries were blurry. I had a pre-surgery appointment with him, and he asked me about my past medical history.

"Nothing!" I answered. "I'm the healthiest person in the world."

Unaware of how harsh he came across, he snorted. "Yeah, right. You *used* to be."

The words slapped my soul, but I was still protected by a layer of numbness until later that night, when it hit me. "I am a patient with cancer. This stamp will forever be on my medical record, and I will never again be able to say that I'm completely healthy."

I didn't cry, but I allowed myself to assimilate that and dwell on it. Then I did what I usually advised my patients to do and grabbed my journal to write a letter of complaint to the Universe. It helped tremendously.

Over the next year, I navigated three cancer surgeries, chemotherapy, radiation, reconstruction, and recovery. I'm still on hormone therapy, living with the knowledge that a recurrence could happen one day. How have I applied what I preach into living with this diagnosis? Let's explore that in this chapter.

NAVIGATING THE GRIEF CYCLE

My story illustrates several of the concepts we've discussed in this book. The first is a refresher of the stages you'll probably go through after receiving life-changing news. Denial, sadness, anger, bargaining, and acceptance are not a continuum but phases you cycle through. Moments of denial allow you a respite to gather strength. But the path to acceptance begins when the numbness breaks and you absorb what's going on. It takes practice, but you can become an expert on using mood swings to your advantage. In the section "Riding the waves," a little later in this chapter, I'll explain how.

CHOOSING TO LIVE IN HEALTHY DENIAL: REFUSING LABELS

Unhealthy denial, pretending nothing is happening, doesn't work well or for long. First, it can lead to neglect and cause dangerous treatment delays; second, our minds are not really at peace. They're still worrying and suffering under the surface. However, when living with a chronic condition, I'm a firm believer in *healthy denial*.

What do I mean by healthy denial? My favorite quote by Norman

Cousins says, "Don't deny the diagnosis. Defy the verdict." Healthy denial means working toward improving the health condition but refusing to identify with it.

For example, let's take type-2 diabetes. Instead of thinking, "I am a diabetic," practicing healthy denial would imply holding a more empowering thought:

"I am not 'a diabetic'—I'm a human being who happens to have diabetes."

Or even better: "I'm a human being *currently* dealing with a blood sugar disorder. My doctor calls it diabetes, but I reserve my right to keep a corner of hope in my heart that my body might regain balance in the future if I make changes like losing weight. In the meantime, I'll take my medication and monitor my blood sugar diligently."

(A note from the doctor: this is not lying. Even the worst medical conditions enter spontaneous remissions sometimes.)

Healthy denial can transform your quality of life. I've consistently witnessed that when a patient fixates on a diagnosis, their symptoms amplify, and when they stop focusing on it, their symptoms improve drastically. I've even seen autoimmune disorders enter remission after a patient decides to focus on enjoying life and stop thinking about the disease—which makes sense, since the immune system is tightly connected to our stress levels. The bottom line: your mind is powerful. Be very careful what thoughts you feed it.

And let's face it, physicians are often wrong. And even when they're right making a diagnosis, they can't predict the future. *Nobody* knows the future, and expecting the worst accomplishes nothing, so there's no point in fretting.

I've chosen to live in healthy denial regarding my twins' special needs. More than one well-intentioned expert has dropped a horrible statistic my way, predicting that my child has a low chance of ever becoming employable or self-sufficient. I nod politely and deep inside ruminate over a few cuss words while thinking, *That's just your opinion. And we're going to prove you wrong.*

Healthy denial becomes the most critical if your doctor has made the cringe-worthy rookie mistake of trying to predict how long you're expected to live. That is something doctors almost always get wrong. If the words *incurable* and *lethal* have been thrown into the mix, simply nod politely while refusing to believe that part. (Still, I recommend you read the section in the next chapter, "Facing Death.")

In summary, we're better off acknowledging the diagnosis, feeling our disappointment about it, *and then releasing it.* When we face a chronic illness, that's something we have to do over and over again—like keeping a house clean, a job that never ends but gets easier with practice.

REMEMBER THE CHRONIC-ISSUES TRIAD: ACCEPTANCE, MOOD VIGILANCE, AND LIVING IN THE NOW

Returning to the story of my breast cancer diagnosis, it illustrates another point that is a critical component of dealing with a chronic illness: Radical Acceptance. We first have to accept what's happening, *so we can let it go.* We must arrive at that point when we say, "This sucks, but I embrace it and will learn to live with it." Please refer to Chapter 13 if you need to remember the components of living with a chronic issue. For acute exacerbations, you can find more resources in Chapter 12.

From heart disease to renal failure to autoimmune disorders to alcoholism, living with a chronic illness will require constant mood vigilance and a commitment to stay in the present moment—keeping our minds from traveling to imaginary grim futures. In the first part of the book, we discussed useful tools, such as reconnecting with your Mood Thermostat and stacking on joy-generating activities as needed. I've tried all those tools on myself and can give testimony: Yes, they also work for a bad health diagnosis.

In this section, let's put those tools in use and combine them with others.

MOOD VIGILANCE TOOLS APPLIED TO LIVING WITH A CHRONIC HEALTH CONDITION:

Have two journals. This was the first piece of advice I gave my oncology patients, and the first thing I did after my diagnosis. I recommend you do it too: Get not one but TWO journals. Label one of them as "Sunny Days Journal." In it, focus on your gratitude exercises (unless you already have a gratitude journal) and write on the days you're feeling okay. How do you think we label the other journal? "Rainy days?" No. I used to get a smile out of my patients when I informed them the title was the *Bitching*

Journal. That's the journal for venting, panicking, dreading, and engaging in catastrophic thinking. There's only one rule: whenever you finish venting your negativity, anger, sadness, disappointment, or fear there, return to your Sunny Days Journal and leave the exercise on a positive note. Make a gratitude entry, a list of sensory things you enjoy (see Chapter 7), or a lesson you're learning that we'll help you in the future—if you're already arriving at epiphanies.

Do you really need two journals? Not really. You could use one for both tasks. However, I recommend the physical act of separating the bad days for three reasons.

1. It gives you permission to really get nasty and real in your venting if you don't run into a page where you've just written about what's right in your life.

2. After a while, I joke that we pour so much negativity on the Bitching Journal that it becomes radioactive, and it's better to keep it out of reach while we're not using it. (In real life, it's not radioactive, but we might develop a Pavlovian negative association when seeing it.)

3. If you're like me and enjoy symbolic ceremonies, keeping that journal allows you to create a ritual later to get rid of it, symbolizing the end of an era or a new commitment to find a new normal in life. Later on, you can choose to burn it, rip it apart, or shred it and then spread the remainders into the ocean—whatever you want. In my experience, it truly feels as if we're committing to leaving the sad memories behind. By the way, I also recommend that strategy if there is a particular person or experience in life you need to debrief to get to forgiveness.

Check the Mood Thermostat regularly. While you're dealing with a long-term health issue, it's more important than ever to avoid dissociation and stay present, to process what's going on. Do you remember the chapter about reconnecting? I recommend asking yourself every day, ideally several times a day, "How do I feel right now, from minus ten to positive ten."

Dial your emotions. You have the control. Adjust your feelings as needed by using your list of favorite mood-booster strategies you put together in the

Joy Diet chapters. You'll be most productive in a 7-9 range. Any time you're at 6 or less, do one of the pleasant activities on your lists to lift you up. If you find yourself with a very low or negative score, it's advisable to grab the Bitching Journal and vent first before attempting any mood-lifting activity.

You might be thinking that it's easier said than done, and you're right. When we're feeling down, it's hard to find the energy to do anything. That's why I recommend you do some venting first (even EFT if you find yourself stuck). Then, pick up one of the easiest brain-disconnecting, Mind Candy activities (especially one that makes you laugh out loud).

Something that helps me get started when I decide to change my mood is watching my body. Are you slouching or slumping? Stand up straight and pull those shoulders back. Are you breathing shallowly? Start taking deep breaths.

Aim for 7-9. When I recommend aiming for a 7-9 on the scale of joy, I don't mean it's bad to be at 10. But I mark it as less than ideal because, in my experience, euphoria during a scary diagnosis often heralds that denial has peaked. Euphoria signals that a bubble is about to burst and send us spiraling down.

Would I recommend that you do something to bring yourself down if you're at a ten? Heck no. Ride it! Milk it! *Store it!* I believe that we have storage compartments of joy in our soul we can tap into later, so use the extra energy of those moments to get momentum on what you want to do and collect moments of joy and pleasure with your loved ones.

Ride the waves. Then, when/if the bubble bursts and you find yourself feeling down, ride that too. Use it as your chance to drain the abscess by venting, processing the emotions, and generating catharsis. You'll be surprised how restorative this system can be. Ride the highs and float with the lows, using each extreme to propel you in the right direction of healing and growth.

Manage the fears. If, at any given time, your predominant feeling is fear or anxiety, you can vent about your fears. Often putting them in black and white helps us put them in perspective. Then, after you've vented enough, focus on joy activities that bring you inner peace. Prayer, meditation,

D Pichardo-Johansson, MD

and love therapy (spending time with loved ones) seem to work best in my experience. Other options include listening to soothing music and indulging in a bittersweet book or movie.

Keep yourself in the present moment. Fast-forwarding to the future helps no one—unless you're consciously using the Time Machine approach to remind yourself to appreciate the present more deeply. Take life one breath at a time. It doesn't matter if there are a hundred (or a million) things that could go wrong tomorrow. They haven't happened yet. And worrying about them is not going to help. If they end up not happening, we worried for nothing. And if they do occur for real, then we wasted precious time worrying when we should've been deeply enjoying *these* days or months of peace before "whatever bad thing" arrives.

REMEMBER THE BOUNCING BACK MINDSET TRIAD. SELF-COMPASSION, PERSPECTIVE, AND WILLINGNESS TO LEARN FROM THE EXPERIENCE.

When you're dealing with a long-term issue taking a toll on your body, treat yourself kindly. Cut yourself slack. Forgive yourself if you've ever been "less than perfect" managing your condition. Pamper yourself as needed.

Then, remember to have perspective: I bet you that somewhere in the world, there is someone who has the same condition, but much, much worse. And I don't mean we'll use that to rejoice over someone else's troubles, but to re-center on gratitude. We'll use it to remind ourselves that it could've been worse—much worse.

Make it a habit to ask yourself regularly, "What have I learned today?" This is particularly helpful when we're recovering from acute exacerbations of a chronic issue.

Refer to Chapter 9 if you need a refreshing course on the mindset of bouncing back.

CAN A BETTER ATTITUDE TRULY IMPACT MY PROGNOSIS?

I've always said the best health booster in the world is wanting to be alive.

The following examples are based on cancer patients, mostly because that was the bulk of the patients I saw. However, the concepts can apply to any chronic issue you face.

Early in my oncology career, I observed that the single strongest predictor of survival in my patients was their absolute commitment to the treatment because they had strong reasons to be alive. I could write another book with the stories of patients who hung on to life way past what doctors predicted because they had a milestone they strongly wanted to reach. Consider my patient Susan, who had small cell lung cancer (a very fast-growing type) and was not responding to treatment. I secretly suspected she only had days to weeks to live and was easing into a talk about hospice when she declared, "Well, doctor, my daughter just announced that she's pregnant. I can't die until she gives birth, and I get to meet my grandkid." She pleasantly shocked her family and me by keeping her word.

And I'm not only talking about prolonging life a few months. Take my patient Cynthia, who had stage IV lung cancer and refused to die for years until both of her teenage sons were settled into a career track. Or my patient Ella, who broke the record of living with metastatic colon cancer because she was enjoying life too much to let go.

If a good attitude toward cancer can make a difference, imagine what it can do for less severe diagnoses.

Even the most skeptical and no-nonsense doctor would agree that a strong desire to live will, at least, ensure compliance with treatment, improving the prognosis. But I believe it goes beyond that. It's very scientifically possible that a strong will to get better can generate yet unknown neurotransmitters and hormone signals that can keep the patient alive and healthy longer—either by regulating the immune system or improving cell regeneration. What's more, the explanation might be deeper than the cellular level, at the atomic and quantum levels. Who knows the interactions our feelings have on our electromagnetic fields? And don't get me started on healing energy and that four-letter word, *the soul*. The topic is so complex I would need to write a whole different book (and I may).

Whatever the potential mechanism, it makes sense to maximize our odds by ensuring an authentic, strong will to live—making sure life is as pleasurable and pleasant as possible. Even if you don't buy into my theory of improved survival, it makes logical sense that successfully navigating the highs and lows would make it easier to stick to treatment or therapy, improving the outcome.

BEING A CAREGIVER

Few life challenges are more painful than seeing someone we love in pain or in danger. I can tell you that learning about my mother's cancer diagnosis was a thousand times more painful and scary than learning about my own. Also, none of my hospitalizations for cancer surgery left the painful mark on my soul that my daughter's hospitalizations did. If you're currently the caregiver of a loved one who's sick, there's an urgent issue you need to tend to, for the love of that person.

Are you ready?

NEVER FORGET TO TAKE CARE OF YOURSELF.

Being a caregiver requires tons of energy transfer. We infuse our ill loved ones with our optimism when they're down. We infuse them with our peace when they're anxious. We infuse them with our enthusiasm when they doubt. You can't do that unless *you* are well charged, and the more you recharge yourself, the more you'll have to give.

Use the Time Travel tool to stay in the now and remember: nothing lasts forever. Sometime in the future, when/if your loved one is not around anymore, you'll look back at these days and miss them. Treasure every moment you have with them and collect memories together.

FINAL WORDS

If you're facing a chronic or life-threatening diagnosis—from cancer to fibromyalgia to substance use disorder—I encourage you even more to apply the exercises in this book. Best-case scenario, an improved emotional state may even help prolong your life. The worst-case scenario, it will make whatever life you have more joyful and worth living. I'll take that any day.

23
FACING DEATH

WHEN SOMEONE YOU LOVE DIES

THERE'S NO RIGHT WAY TO lose a loved one. A sudden loss that catches us completely off guard can be devastating. On the other hand, losing someone from a slow, protracted illness may allow us to say goodbye, yet will likely leave us drained and exhausted.

Losing someone we love is heartbreaking, even in the best of circumstances. What do I mean by "best circumstances?" When we face the natural death of an elder who enjoyed a full life, and believe that death is not the end, but as a transition. Even if you have that type of faith and your loved one died peacefully in their sleep at age ninety, you'll still grieve as you say goodbye to them and a stage of your life.

Imagine how much harder it is in less than ideal situations. For example, when our loved one dies prematurely, from tragic circumstances, or when we don't have the consolation of life after death beliefs. Or when we arrived at our loved one's death worn out by years of witnessing them decline.

When someone you love dies, you have to allow yourself to embrace your grief before you can find gratitude again. To speed up that process, here are a couple of tools that have helped me tremendously at times of loss. The first tool worked miracles in the life of hundreds of cancer patients and their relatives I cared for as a hematologist-oncologist. It's a tool we discussed in Chapter 19, where we used it for heartbreak. Here we'll apply it to loss: The Goodbye Letter.

TOOL #1 THE GOODBYE LETTER

Whether your loved one died suddenly or slowly, by the time they pass on, chances are you've been running on adrenaline for weeks—starting with hectic hospital admissions and ending with funeral arrangements. It's difficult to assimilate what's happening until much later. Perhaps, you couldn't be present at the moment of their death. And even if you were fortunate enough to be there, the goodbye might've been butchered or dampened by your loved one's altered mental status. You (and your loved one's spirit) deserve a proper goodbye.

Like I used to instruct my patients and their relatives, I encourage you to write a long letter to the person you lost. In it, you'll say everything you wished you'd said to them and didn't have a chance. I firmly believe that our loved ones do have a chance to listen. Devoid of the ego, they can now deeply understand where we come from and love us better than ever—even if we need to express resentment.

Start the letter by venting your sadness, and then make sure to cover anger, fear, and regret. Cry if needed—wail, sob, heave. Express your anger: cuss if needed; send a letter to God's complaint department protesting the unfairness of having to lose your loved one or having seen them suffer. Acknowledge grudges and resentments you had with them and never grieved. Ask for their forgiveness for anything you feel you did to hurt them. Allow yourself to feel the fear you suppressed while having to deal with their illness or death. (In my case, grieving my mother included the fear of having inherited a cancer gene from her and getting cancer someday.) Write about your regrets—everything you wished you could've done and didn't. In my case, my biggest regrets were that my mother would never get to meet her grandchildren—something she dreamed of.

This exercise can be intense, and of course, if you don't feel safe at any time, reach for help. You may need to take breaks and return to it later. But please finish it. Make sure you have squeezed the last drop of feelings left to express and then, as the last step, finish the letter with *gratitude*.

Thank your loved one for everything they gave you. Remember everything they taught you, all the moments they were there for you, all the love they gave you. When you have run out of grateful memories with them, end the letter with the sentence. "Thank you for everything you brought into my life. Now I release you to continue your journey. Now I let you go."

When you're done with that, hold on to the gratitude. You will need it for the next steps.

TOOL #2 INTENSE GRATITUDE

If you were blessed enough to have a great relationship with your loved one and don't have many grievances to forgive or unfinished business, you might find yourself arriving at this point faster. This proved to be true for me with my parents.

This is the ninja version of "It could've been worse." In this exercise, we deeply acknowledge that we were never entitled to whatever small amount of time we had with our loved one and that every day with them was a gift. I can illustrate this in both an expected and an unexpected loss.

My mother: When my mother was diagnosed with incurable cancer at age forty-seven and died at age fifty-one, I often reminded myself of a story my grandmother used to tell me. My mother had fallen ill with diphtheria, a life-threatening pediatric infection, at age one. She'd proven allergic to penicillin, the only treatment available back then, and the town doctor (their rural town didn't even have a hospital) had told my grandmother that her baby would most likely die. Grandma spent all night rocking my mother in her arms at home while she gasped for air. She was convinced that Mom surviving that illness had been a miracle.

Around the time of my mother's diagnosis and death, I kept repeating to myself, "Thank you, God. If she would've died at age one, I would've never had her as a mother. Thank you, God, because she had those extra fifty years, I had the privilege of having her for over twenty."

My father: When my father died suddenly, he was a couple of months short of his sixty-eighth birthday and in amazing health, riding bicycling marathons. His accidental death came as a blow.

The day of his funeral service, many people stood and praised the exceptional man he'd been, especially for the Dominican culture. Listening to them talk, I thought about all those people who had the traditional

Dominican *paterfamilias* as a father—a violent alcoholic or chronic cheater. I also thought about so many friends whose fathers had been workaholic businessmen who never had time for their families. When it was my turn to speak, a crystal-clear inspiration filled me. "Thank you, God, for the years I had my father. It may look as if I was cheated of time, but the truth is that he was the extreme example of quality instead of quantity. He gave me more love in the thirty-seven years I had him than many fathers give their children in a hundred years."

IN SUMMARY

The key to healing after a loved one's death will always be time. But we can help speed up the process by ensuring we say a proper goodbye. Shifting from grief to gratitude requires acknowledging that we were never entitled to anything and every minute we had them in our lives was a gift.

WHEN YOU OR SOMEONE YOU LOVE HAS BEEN DIAGNOSED WITH A TERMINAL ILLNESS

First, allow me to get something out of the way: doctors are wrong all the time, and we should always reserve the right to doubt their predictions. I encourage you to read the previous chapter, where I go into much more detail about that and the topic of healthy denial. But for this section, I'll work on the assumption that the "death sentence" is real.

I admit it: being diagnosed with a lethal illness sucks so much, little anyone can say will seem to help. I know that because *I lived it*.

A few days after my first of three breast cancer surgeries, I received a shocking surprise from my pathology report. I'd chosen to have bilateral mastectomies, thinking that way I would not have to deal with the stress of finding a positive margin and having to return to the OR. I never expected the pathology to describe a "distant metastasis to skin." Because I was an oncologist, I knew exactly what that meant with little room for denial: If the cancer had spread to skin far away, it meant the cancer cells had already seeded through the blood to many other places. The cancer had been upgraded to stage IV, labeled incurable.

Like my mother used to say, "It's not the same calling the devil as seeing him arrive." I had dealt with hundreds (probably thousands) of stage IV cancer patients by then. I had cheered them up with speeches about faith and living one day at a time. Yet when it was my turn to face the possibility of not being there for my children as they grew up, I felt terrified.

Still, I will share with you the before and after speech I used to give patients:

MY PEP TALK TO PATIENTS FACING A TERMINAL DIAGNOSIS (BEFORE I LIVED IT)

Here I share the pep talk I used to give patients after breaking the news that their disease was likely to be fatal. I still consider it quite good:

"Yes, your disease is incurable *as of the current state of science*—there is always the possibility that a cure might be discovered in your lifetime, and it's all a matter of hanging on long enough."

Here I must add, I wasn't bluffing. I'd seen science advance enough just in the decade and a half I practiced to see previously incurable cancer diagnoses transformed to curable or practically curable (kept under control enough that patients could die of old age). That included my mother's illness, multiple myeloma. It also included the discovery of immunotherapy for melanoma and the revolution of TKI therapy for chronic myelogenous leukemia.

Next, I would tell the patients: "And even if they don't discover a cure for your illness and you do die from it, here's the truth: We are *all* going to die. I'm standing here in front of you, completely healthy, and I may cross the street tomorrow and be run over by a truck—and *you* end up going to *my* funeral."

(That's also true).

"Every single person on this planet will die someday," I would continue, "and you have received the mixed blessing of *getting a little notice in advance*. This is your chance to make sure you tend to your unfinished business. Make a bucket list and see which of the dreams you haven't pursued yet are still doable. Call anybody you love and haven't talked to in a while and tell them you love them. Call anybody with whom you have an unresolved grudge and work it out now. Also, tend to the practical things: make a living will, organize your estate…

"Only God knows how long you (or I, or anybody) will live. All you can control is enjoying each day to the maximum, like they say, hoping for the best while preparing for the worst. Like my favorite saying goes, 'Dream like you're going to live forever, live like you only have today.'" (By the way, I plagiarized myself and placed those words on the lips of my fictional character Dr. Joy Clayton in my first mystery/romantic suspense book, *Beyond Physical*.)

THE REAL STUFF (MY SPEECH AFTER I EXPERIENCED THE SCARE OF A DEATH SENTENCE)

All that eventually helped me when I had to face an uncertain future. But I admit it can all be cold comfort when denial wears off and depression sets in.

Do you want to know *the only thing* that *really* helped me, in practicality, when it was my turn to face a life-threatening diagnosis? Only ONE thing soothed that pain. Are you ready to hear it?

Drumroll, please.

It is *faith*.

If you or someone you love face a death sentence, the only thing that will relieve your pain is reconnecting to your spirituality—whatever form that takes. Honestly, the whole brevity of human life makes absolutely no sense unless we approach it with a spiritual view. Compared to the billions of years the universe has been around, what is one hundred years, but a flash?

Nobody can claim to understand what happens after death. I've met a few people who've had near-death experiences, and they describe very similar feelings but differ in the experience details. Two women from different spiritual backgrounds saw different beings greeting them. Yet they both described the same feeling of complete peace, love, and understanding that they were "returning home."

That's an image that seemed to make a huge difference to many of my patients and their relatives when they were facing the end of life. Remember, this is just a vacation trip. We are not our bodies. We're souls that temporarily put on a spacesuit of flesh to come to this adventure. And now, at the end of the journey, we take off our suits and return home. We might feel some nostalgia about what we leave behind, and we certainly may feel a little sad that our vacation is coming to an end. But we're mostly happy because *we're going home.*

Trying to wrap our brains around death beyond that concept is "troubling our pretty little minds." Every other supportive evidence I've found is all theoretical exercise: Doesn't it seem absurd that this bright consciousness I am, able to encompass the whole universe in a thought, would be around only for a handful of years? When I think of my departed loved ones—my mother, my father, my grandma—don't I vividly feel they're not really gone? Doesn't my love for those who've left before me keep flowing? And don't I clearly feel that love is going *somewhere*, being received and returning to me, making me feel it is not true that they've ceased to exist?

So no, we don't know exactly what will happen after death. But I have noticed that I live the most peaceful and joyful life when I choose to believe that death is not the end, even if I have no clue what comes afterward. Is there a literal heaven with pearly gates and angels singing? Is there a pleasure-filled paradise where we eat everything we want without gaining weight and download all the knowledge we always craved from celestial libraries? Do we all go to sleep and only wake up at the time of the final judgment? Is there literal reincarnation? Does our ego just disappear, and we become blissful, mindless energy flowing through every molecule of the multiverses?

I don't know. But my trip here is much more enjoyable when I don't allow nihilistic thoughts to spoil it. And *just in case* what happens after death is something completely different from the pleasures of the flesh, I will remind myself every day to treasure every bit of my human experience.

In the long-term, having faith is the only way to live. After all, repeating the obvious: we are all going to die sooner or later. We have to radically accept that.

That's the way I live. After three cancer surgeries, chemotherapy, radiation, and hormone therapy I must take every day for at least ten years, I've chosen to believe that I'm cancer-free. Back then, we concluded the skin metastasis was actually a second, ectopic breast cancer (a rare condition where breast cancer rises on the skin). I know some of my doctors are not that convinced. Only time will tell. In the meanwhile, I'm aware that my stay on this planet is finite, and I'm committed to making the best out of it.

EPILOGUE

"Living is beautiful. I love everything life offers me.
Pleasure restores me; pain strengthens me."

(Que bello es vivir. El Kanka,
Spanish singer and songwriter.)

IF YOU TAKE A MOMENT to reflect on the stunning complexity of the universe and nature, you'll agree that it's difficult not to be impressed. From the greatness of a galaxy to the inconceivable minuteness of an atom; from the astonishing diversity of different life forms to the recurrent themes of life cycles and human experiences—whatever the intelligence or "software" running the show, it seems to know what it's doing.

Consider one of my favorite topics: Our body systems, our organs, our tissues, our cells. The human body is a miracle we've grown so accustomed to that we forget to appreciate it until something malfunctions. But how perfectly it works most of the time.

Yes. *Life* is amazing. After fifteen years practicing oncology and facing death every day, I learned the most important lesson about living: The biggest tragedy that can happen to someone is *not* dying but *failing to live wholeheartedly*. Life is only worth living with passion—no lukewarm hearts allowed, please.

Live fully. However you define joy, embrace it. Sometimes, you'll also have to face a broken heart or lost dream, but that's part of life's richness. Because if the price to pay to be pain-free is living in anesthesia—also missing the happiness—it's not worth it.

Welcome the whole range of human emotions. Embrace sadness as the way to heal. Embrace anger as the force needed to make a change. Embrace fear as our indicator of vulnerability. Embrace regret as the teacher that reminds you to seize the moment. But always return to joy. Joy allows us to master the other feelings and gives us the fuel to serve the world.

Be generous, sharing your joy. Like love, the more you spread, the more you'll receive. And that includes being kind and loving to yourself. We're all connected. When you make yourself happy, you're adding to the positive balance in the happiness bank account of all of humanity. And the more love and patience you give yourself, the stronger you'll be to take care of others.

Difficult and wonderful things intertwine in every moment of our lives, like wheat and tares growing together in a field. If we try to rip out the bad ones, we risk also uprooting the good ones. To allow both to coexist without spoiling our harvest, we must give more of our attention to nurturing the good parts. By all means, don't covet someone else's life and don't wish to push the fast-forward button to speed over a challenge. If we could get rid of what's bothering us right now, we will, for sure, realize we left behind something we'll miss forever.

I want to leave you with one last thought—the same words I sent to my oncology patients in the goodbye letter I mailed when I left my job: "If there's something I learned from my patients in the past years is that life is short; that we must pursue happiness for as brief or as long as our stay on this planet is; and that in the end, we don't regret what we did, but what we didn't do. May you always live by those mottos. And may you always remember that the best health booster is wanting to be alive."

NOTE FROM THE AUTHOR

Dear Reader:

It is an honor for me that you took the time to read this book. I hope you found it helpful and entertaining. If you enjoyed it, please take a moment to recommend it to a friend or leave a review.

Yet, nothing compares to one-on-one work. I'll be happy to personally help you apply and individualize these strategies. I can also help you clarify what you want, create goals aligned with your values, and support you on the journey to achieve them. Whether your goal is reinventing yourself completely or just becoming a better, happier version of yourself, I have many more tools and strategies to help than the ones that appear in this book. For a complimentary session, please visit my website at www.joyfullysuccessful.com

Please also feel free to email me at pichardojohanssonmd@gmail.com—I'm a busy lady, but I'll do my best to answer all emails.

Thank you again for reading.

Love,
Diely

JOIN MY NEWSLETTER!

For an extensive list of sensorial ideas to create your joy generating activity join my newsletter: https://mailchi.mp/f581a47174e1/bouncing-back

You'll receive the expanded list in PDF format so you can print it or save it for future use. You'll also receive:

1- Sneak Peeks on new projects
2- Opportunities to read and review future books for free
3- Exclusive material, including fiction, non-fiction, and creative non-fiction

Join now! https://mailchi.mp/f581a47174e1/bouncing-back

ABOUT THE AUTHOR

Dr. Pichardo-Johansson is a retired physician, Life Coach, and author of nine books. After fifteen years practicing oncology and becoming a cancer survivor herself, she decided she no longer wanted to make a living fighting death. Instead, she now teaches people to fully enjoy life. She specializes in helping professional women find authentic joy and love, and helping clients reinvent themselves after life-shaking events.

Dr. Pichardo-Johansson is a Summa Cum Laude graduate who obtained her Medical Degree at *Pontificia Universidad Católica Madre y Maestra* Dominican Republic. She completed an Internal Medicine residency at Wayne State University in Detroit and a Hematology-Oncology fellowship and masters in clinical investigation at Northwestern University/ Northwestern Memorial Hospital in Chicago. She received her Life Coach Certification from the Robbins-Madanes/Strategic Intervention Center.

She's had a lifelong interest in personal development, mind-body-spirit medicine, and the healing powers of love and laughter. Her mottos are "The best medicine is a strong desire to be alive" and "The biggest tragedy is not death—it's failing to live with passion." Her passions include music , traveling and fiction writing. She has published eight romance and mystery novels.

Dr. Pichardo-Johansson lives in Melbourne Beach, Florida, with her soulmate husband and her four beloved children, including twins with special needs.